When
Suffering
Persists

When Suffering Persists

Frederick W. Schmidt

MOREHOUSE PUBLISHING

Copyright © 2001 by Frederick W. Schmidt

Morehouse Publishing
P.O. Box 1321
Harrisburg, PA 17105

Morehouse Publishing is a division of the Morehouse Group.

With one exception, the names of people whose stories appear in this book have been changed.

Printed in the United States of America

Cover design by Trude Brummer

Cataloging-in-Publication data is available from
the Library of Congress
ISBN 0-8192-1829-4

01 02 03 04 05 06   10 9 8 7 6 5 4 3 2 1

This book is lovingly dedicated
to Elaine and Lindsay

and
in memory of

John Krauss

Joseph Melotti

Charlotte Quinn

Dominic Ruggeroli

Pauline Schmidt

Samuel Vaughn

May light perpetual shine upon them.

Contents

Acknowledgments

This book is the product of relationships, reflected in the stories told, the thoughts shared, and the words used. Whatever might be of value in it can be traced to the richness of those friendships. Whatever remains amiss can be traced to my own limited ability to give that richness life and shape.

It is sent on its way with thanks to many who are unnamed, but who discussed their ideas in churches and classrooms; their thoughts are reflected here. There are still others who can and should be mentioned. My thanks to the people of St. Stephen's Cathedral, Harrisburg, Pennsylvania, who heard the first version of the thoughts discussed here; Ed Seay, who first encouraged me to find a publisher and then inquired (again and again) about my progress; Lee Jefferson, who assisted me with some of the research; David Schlafer, who read one of the later versions of the manuscript, gave thoughtful advice, and has been a valued conversation partner; Val Gittings, who read an earlier version of the manuscript and critiqued it; Lauren Cusick, who demonstrated a capacity for grace and good work under pressure; Corey Kent and Trude Brummer, who brought artistry to the book; Debra Farrington, who as an editor has been all that a writer could hope for; and Elaine and Lindsay, whose love sustains me.

CHAPTER ONE

Having Suffered
My Stories, Yours, and Ours

Suffering passes. Having suffered never passes.
—Charles Péguy[1]

I experienced a number of childhood surgeries, bumps, and
bruises, but my first conscious encounter with suffering took
place in late adolescence. I had spent four years on our debate
team. During most of that time we had just enough money to
compete in a county-wide forensics league that included high
schools from my hometown of Louisville, Kentucky. Late in
my senior year, however, we were finally able to convince our
school's principal to give us enough money to enter an invita-
tional tournament being held in nearby Bardstown.

On the morning of the tournament four of us set out on
snow-covered roads in a car driven by our coach and teacher,
Sara Edison. Kentucky roads are hazardous in the snow, in large
part because we have one and only one solution for them—
spring. The going was slow. We slipped gently into a ditch early
in the drive out of town and then, much more tentatively, we
continued our progress south.

I have retrograde amnesia, but according to witnesses, with
half of the trip behind us, Sara lost control of the car and we
fishtailed into a head-on collision with a two-and-a-half-ton
truck. The results were devastating. The much larger truck
ripped into the front of the car, carrying glass and metal ahead

of it. Injured in a way that no one could effectively help her, our young teacher and friend died en route to the small hospital in Bardstown. The rest of us were examined and then transported back to a hospital in Louisville.

Carried along by adrenaline and shielded from the realities by shock, I continued to function as if nothing had happened. As a result, I insisted on riding in the passenger seat of the ambulance in order to make room in the back for my friends. It was only after we arrived back in Louisville that the physicians discovered the full extent of my injuries.

Admitted to the same hospital where I had worked as a volunteer, I spent twenty-eight days under close medical care and scrutiny. Then I returned home to a succession of hospital beds, wheelchairs, casts, crutches, and back and leg braces. Winter gave way to spring and my senior year in high school gave way to my freshman year of college before I left most of the visible evidence of the accident behind me.

The Autobiographical Nature of Suffering

Just exactly what I make of this experience and experiences like them is something that I hope to explore with you. In part, I mention a story of my own in order to underline the fact that the conversation we are embarking on cannot be and should not be objectified. Suffering is ultimately neither academic nor abstract for you, or for me. It is inevitably a part of everyone's emotional, spiritual, and intellectual pilgrimage; and the conversation we will have between the covers of this book is not a conversation at the end of that pilgrimage, but somewhere en route.

I've also begun with one of my own experiences, as you should with yours, because suffering has an irreducibly autobiographical character that cannot be neglected. What we suffer and the way in which we experience it is like a kaleidoscope that consists of a hundred and one pieces of colored glass that refract the light in differing ways as we turn the lens. The character of our pain or loss, the shapes of our personalities, and the textures of our lives at any one point along the way will give a subtle but significant shading to even common experiences. A small child who is told there are people in other parts of the world who would like her spinach finds small comfort in that appeal to the greater suffering of others. Like her, we want to know if we can box up the experience and send it on its way—FedEx or UPS?

Accommodating the Experience of Others

On another level, however, in the course of our conversation we will find that the experience of others is of enormous relevance. The pain and loss experienced by others reminds us that whatever we may offer by way of explanation for the problem of suffering, we will need to do more than accommodate our own experience, or a single moment in that experience.

Over and over again I am struck by the ease with which we generalize from the events in our own lives. Those who experience infertility may interpret their experience as divine prompting to adopt an orphan. Those who experience infertility as utter and complete loss may feel very differently. Those who quickly find new employment in the wake of a layoff may see their good fortune as an answer to prayer. Those who slip into long-term unemployment may define God's care in very different terms, focusing instead on the insights they gain into themselves, their sense of self-worth, and the values that shape their lives. Whatever the experience, these and other elements of our lives are often woven into the fabric of a life narrative that acquires nuance and focus with telling and retelling the story. They can also determine the way in which we understand the experiences of others who encounter the same kind of loss.

This kind of generalization is a natural and necessary part of making sense out of life. Arguably the best kind of therapy is, in fact, just that—the task of telling our story, of putting the pieces into a larger narrative. We do it instinctively and with good reason. The ability to explore and articulate the meaning of our lives distinguishes us from other parts of creation.

But the generalizations we make based on those life stories do not necessarily take the needs of others into account; and when the generalizations harden into propositions, the danger of failing to allow for the complexity of human experience grows exponentially. We cite the close calls and perceived deliverances that we experience as testimony to God's goodness and as answers to our prayers without ever taking into account the implications those assertions may have for those who are not delivered, or who continue to suffer. When we do fail to take the complexity of human experience into account, it is left up to those who continue to suffer to make sense of the disparity between their experience and ours.

Again, an example from my own life will help to illustrate what I mean. My wife Elaine and I were married shortly after we graduated from college in 1975. We planned to have children, but like many young married couples paying school bills, we felt it was unwise to start a family immediately. Apart from the question of finances, we had a number of friends with children who were seminary-bound. We could see how difficult it is to maintain the quality of family life that we felt was important for a child while juggling the financial and academic demands of a seminary education. In addition, Elaine hoped to work on her master's degree and this seemed as good a time as any to pursue those avenues of training and service. So, we postponed starting our family, never dreaming what little bearing those decisions had on the future.

Graduate work proved to be every bit as demanding as we expected and seminary gave way to two years of teaching Greek and plans for my part to do doctoral work, and so—with good reason—we waited for a total of five years before we were ready to have a child. Then, in 1980 we moved to Great Britain. We decided that although doctoral work was not likely to be less demanding than seminary, it was time to consider having a child.

That autumn in Oxford we began to plan for a family and that autumn became, in some ways, the entrance to a long, dark tunnel that stretched out almost six years before us. In late

October of 1980, Elaine became pregnant. We were ecstatic. In late November she miscarried and spent the Thanksgiving holiday in bed. A lack of any further success gave way to appointments with doctors: appointments with doctors gave way to clinics; and the clinics concluded that the infertility problems we faced put the odds at something like one in a thousand that we would ever have our own child.

But even doctors will pursue lost causes, and so their conclusions gave way to more appointments that (on a sporadic basis) gave way to an endless, numbing series of still more appointments and enough temperature charts that, if bound together, would have been the thickness of the *Encyclopedia Britannica*. Those were dark days. Many of them we survived only because the cycle of depression with which we struggled was one in which we were rarely "down" at the same time. I cannot speak for Elaine, but for me anger, bitterness, and bewilderment at the injustice of it all were very much my companions. I became vividly aware of parents who appeared to abuse their children and who appeared to have no real appreciation for what they had. I noticed unwed teenagers with children; I noticed toys and nursery rhymes, other people's daughters and other people's sons.

Then, in 1985, at a time when things were no less depressing and the doctors' predictions were no more encouraging, Elaine conceived and on October 9 of the same year our daughter was born. At the time Lindsay was conceived I was no more hopeful, no less depressed or angry than I had been on the days before she was conceived.

Given the religious climate of our country, I could easily have generalized from our struggle, writing a book that described our experience and the steps that we took to claim a spiritual victory with the birth of our child. There are already a number of similar, very successful books on the market, ones that promise a cookbook remedy to some of life's greater struggles.

But apart from the dishonesty writing such a book would have required, a far larger problem would have been the difficulty of applying that description of our experience to the experience of others. At the time our daughter was born, we knew people of great faith who continued to struggle with identifiable fertility problems, but who were never able to conceive. We knew still other couples who could not conceive, but whose inability to do so did not yield to any easy explanation. There was no clear explanation for our ability, finally, to conceive, and for the inability of others.

Although to generalize from our experience is both natural and, to some extent, necessary, it is also fraught with dangers. Ours is a single lens on life, representative of only a fraction of what might happen to people faced with similar challenges; and that single experience is then refracted by the shape of our own autobiography. Multiply those possibilities by the differences in each of our life circumstances, as well as the differences in each of our life stories, and the number of ways in which our struggles might be different from those of others is almost endless.

Drawing on a single life story and thereby assuming that everyone else sees life in the same way we do, we run the risk of fostering despair and frustration in those we seek to help. Efforts to reassure people of God's care and the comfort to be found in prayer can also lead to discouraging comparisons. The speed with which we recover, and the question of whether we recover at all, can become the engine of still more loss and pain.

Unanswered Questions

Drawing on our own lives alone also raises serious and difficult questions. Are we "blessed" by God when we escape the loss that our neighbor experiences? Are answers to prayer given to one cancer sufferer and not another? Are those who do not recover simply given a different answer to their prayers? Or if others are blessed, does God curse those who do not recover?

What of life's other arenas where persistent suffering takes other forms? Dallas, Texas, is the ninth largest city in the United States. On almost any reading, it is one of our country's economic dynamos. It is also a city of megachurches. The confluence of economic prosperity and religious fervor makes Dallas a place where people tend to attribute their economic fortunes to the hand of God. It is not unusual to hear corporate leaders attribute new clients and larger profit margins to God's hand, or to imply their success is an index of their righteousness. But it is also a city where the average age of those who are homeless is nine. Does God manage the growing success of high-tech industries and neglect children? Do stock options move God in a way that the cries of children do not?

And what about the complexities of suffering in the midst of war? How do we account for the suffering that we escape at the expense of others in times of war and conflict? What does it mean to pray for the defeat or demise of another human being, while raising prayers for our own safety? Do we believe God is clearly the ally of one country and not another? Do we believe there were innocents killed in the London Blitz, but there were no innocent souls in Dresden or Nagasaki?

Often the rhetoric and behavior that characterize war help to give the impression that questions of this kind can be answered with deceptive ease. World War II is an excellent example. The allied forces served well as God's army and Adolf Hitler is, in the minds of many, the incarnation of evil. The war itself can be characterized as a just war. The so-called "final solution" that led to the extermination of millions and Hitler's relentless attacks on Germany's neighbors suggest that this war, at least, was a reasonably obvious conflict in which prayers for deliverance and justification could be clearly focused.

But this is hardly the whole picture. The social and political climate in Germany following World War I helped to create a political and economic climate in which Hitler's rise to power became possible. Rendered poor and impotent by the punitive nature of the Treaty of Versailles, Germans of every faith labored under the hardships created by still another war. Nor were all of Hitler's followers equally culpable. Children and teenagers were slowly recruited to assist in the cause with appeals that exploited both their age and their relative innocence. Even some Jewish Germans found it difficult to believe that Hitler would turn on them.

For our own part, American self-interest delayed our involvement in the war. It prompted our own leaders to ignore early evidence of the systematic extermination of Jews and gypsies. Later the same self-interest led us to bomb civilian population centers in Europe and Japan in an attempt to shorten the war on both the western and eastern fronts.

Now, none of this is necessarily grounds for arguing that any other response was possible. That is an entirely different question that cannot be addressed here. Nor would I want to minimize the hideous nature of the Holocaust. But I do want to underline the character of war and the prayers it elicits as part of the complex landscape we call suffering. The tensions, contradictory behavior, lost innocence, and destruction that mark a conflict of this kind make the question of what is and is not God's will a complex matter. For that reason, the perspective that any one nation had was, at best, a window into a much larger experience that can only be described as a tragedy.

Unacknowledged Suffering

Once we realize that our own experience is an inadequate window into the dynamics of suffering, we are then ready to see that there may be suffering that completely escapes our notice and goes unacknowledged. For example, predominantly white American churches confined to the lenses of our own experience have, at times, been slow to respond to the racism that has inflicted suffering on the African American community for over two centuries.

Indeed, our blindness to that suffering has led to incongruity in our behavior that is stunningly immoral and flies in the face of the gospel's injunction to love our neighbors. When, for example, American congregations were first integrated in the seventeenth and eighteenth centuries, enslaved African Americans were admitted to worship, but only under the strict supervision of their slave masters. Confined to the back of the church, or chained to the floor of a balcony, African Americans were often required to stand through the entire service. They were never allowed to preach, nor were they allowed to receive communion. Any activity that might have placed them at the front of the church was avoided.[2]

Just how little we still understand of the unacknowledged pain that racism inflicts was apparent in the disparate reactions to the trial of O. J. Simpson in 1995. The trial was an unexpected crucible for testing the climate of race relations in the United States; white Americans found it almost impossible to comprehend the reaction of black Americans, when some celebrated the acquittal of a man who many (both white and black) believe is guilty. But what incredulous white Americans overlook is both the history of discrimination and the suffering caused by the continuing "stealth racism" that shapes the African American experience.[3] What appeared to be a question of one man's guilt or innocence was for the African American community a question embedded in much larger patterns of discrimination and injustice. The pain that those patterns had inflicted are still widely unacknowledged, and the surprise expressed by white Americans at the reaction of African Americans is an indication of just how completely that suffering has gone unnoticed.

There are, of course, other kinds of unnoticed and unacknowledged suffering. Differences in economic opportunity cloak the suffering that many people experience on a regular basis. At the middle and upper rungs of our country's economic ladder, it is easy to assume that the ability to make ends meet revolves largely around issues of self-discipline and effort. The suffering that comes with poverty can be either invisible or easily dismissed, based on the assumption that all one need do is find a job. Nothing, of course, could be further from the truth. Training, education, and even mental health can trap those who suffer economic hardship.

Still other kinds of unnoticed and unacknowledged suffering have less to do with social patterns and more to do with our perception of life's events and relationships. The grief that accompanies miscarriage is often easily dismissed and overlooked. We have become so inured to the news of divorce and to the frequency of remarriage that we have started to minimize the pain and suffering that comes with the dissolution of a relationship.

The Layered Complexity of Suffering

As we learn more about the stories of others—stories of family, friends, and those personally unknown to us—we also come face-to-face with the layered complexity of suffering. Suffering has roots that lie beyond the conscious choice of anyone acting out of malice. There are, for example, bureaucratic structures that ensure suffering, even though they are often put in place for the best of reasons.

My wife recently served as an assistant principal at an elementary school in the Metro Washington area, where the average cost of a house is $500,000. But, in her school of 710 little souls, 78 percent of the children received free or reduced-cost lunches. Fifty percent of the entire school population and 70 percent of the kindergarten-age children spoke Spanish as their first language. And because the vast majority of the Spanish-speaking children were refugees from the political strife in parts of Latin America, many of the families had few if any opportunities for education in Spanish, never mind in the English language.

In the autumn of 1997, one of those children, a first-grader from Honduras, entered a school-wide contest to create a picture that would serve as the logo for the school. Miguel focused on the caboose from a train that stood outside the school and served as a distinctive neighborhood landmark. The outline of Miguel's caboose had a charming irregularity that is characteristic of young children, and the bright red that he used to color his picture wandered over the lines. A series of four irregular wheels rode on a small section of track below, and above the caboose was a bright yellow sun that hinted at the light and warmth that we all associate with happy children.

Miguel won the contest. The school framed his drawing and displayed it in the entryway foyer. The picture was used on school T-shirts worn by students, faculty, and administrators, as well as on stationery. But a month after the contest, he and his family were deported and in November of 1998 (just over a year later) Hurricane Mitch ravaged Central America, including the country of Honduras. No one at the school has been able to determine the family's whereabouts, or their fate.

The laws that cut short a happy life in a new home and sent a child back into the path of a hurricane were not designed for that purpose. There were far more impersonal and even legitimate considerations at work. But the unintended consequences for a young Honduran were of tragic proportions. The same could be said of laws that favor the preservation of families but send children back into abusive environments, and provisions that make it profitable to create corporate sweatshops overseas.

The layered complexity of suffering can take other forms, too. In our complex culture the values that shape our society can bring powerful forces to bear on families and individuals, destroying both. Children, for example, labor under the burden of a rising divorce rate. We live in a society that increasingly thinks of divorce as a means of self-actualization and not as a tragedy. We have convinced ourselves that the children can not only survive, but flourish in the wake of divorce, particularly if the parents were unhappy when married. In fact, however, the research indicates otherwise. The children who suffer through divorces struggle to feel loved and secure. They are, at times, the battleground of adult bitterness and they find it difficult to establish lasting relationships of their own as adults.[4]

Women and men also struggle to preserve the fabric of their own lives in the face of growing demands in the workplace. In spite of their efforts, however, an ever increasing number of people are overwhelmed by those challenges. Two-career families struggle to meet growing financial demands, each partner often assuming more than one job. To make ends meet they assume responsibilities that require an inordinate amount of time. They are "'worked' instead of working," driving themselves and their families into lives marked by forms of suffering that we now take for granted, including domestic violence, alcoholism, teenage suicide, and stress-induced illnesses.[5]

Some of the suffering that results has long-term effects. Chronicling the massive layoffs of the mid-1990s, journalist Barbara Rudolf describes the struggle of Tom Chase, who was fired by AT&T when his nine-member division was eliminated in a round of downsizing.[6] Given his experience and position, he could not believe that he would be unable to find comparable employment. But after a brief, part-time job as a consultant and a few months of other work, he was unable to find new employment. It was only after two years and the loss of his family that he began a long process of recovery, taking jobs that paid a small fraction of the salary he once earned.

In other cases the results of similar workplace suffering can be finally devastating. Years ago in a teaching fellowship in Greek, I became friends with one of the students in the class who was only two or three years younger than I was. Samuel and I had a number of good conversations. When I decided to do further graduate work in England, he decided to take an exchange pastorate in Ireland, and we agreed that visiting one another would broaden our experience of the United Kingdom—and save both of us a fair amount of money on meager student budgets. Through the years, we stayed in touch. Samuel returned to the United States and the Pacific Northwest.

As I knew him, Samuel had an enormous capacity for appreciating the smaller things in life. Whatever the challenges, he was engaged by the life of the communities in which he ministered and his hobbies provided a source of diversion wherever he traveled. That was especially helpful in the new work that he chose to do, planting churches on behalf of his denomination. Like many other modern undertakings, church planting is lonely, demanding work. Somewhere along the way, for reasons that no one will probably ever fathom, he lost the capacity to rejoice in the smaller dimensions of his parishioners' lives and in the life-giving dimensions of his family and hobbies. Preoccupied with the goals he had set for the growth of his church, he communicated less often with family and friends. The hobbies and other interests slipped to the margins of his life. Then a brief letter from his wife arrived:

Dear Elaine and Fred,
This letter is to let you know that Samuel took his life last Monday, January 11th. Services were Friday, January 15th. It is a shock to all of us—apparently he was depressed over his work situation, but had not spoken of his pain to anyone. I wanted you to know because you have been part of our lives for many years, and we have shared many things.
Cheryl

The suffering we often experience can arise almost unnoticed from the most familiar patterns of life. Slowly, subtly shaping the world around us, it is much like the air that we breathe. We rarely see the ways our lives are affected until matters have reached crisis proportions and, when we finally recognize the damage done, there is no clear culprit to blame, no easy explanation to give.

The Hidden Complexity of Suffering

It is little wonder that in contemplating the problem of suffering we often gravitate to the examples that can be explained in a more direct fashion, linking human sin and error to the losses we experience. We cite the addict who dies of an overdose, the alcoholic who dies of sclerosis, and the criminal who is convicted of a crime. It is, perhaps, the need for this kind of predictability that is at the heart of our collective passion for civil litigation and capital punishment. To identify culprits and their punishment addresses the deep need we have for order and explanation.

In fact, however, even when a villain appears to provide an explanation for the pain that some endure, we are rarely on ground that is at all simple. Instead, a hidden complexity that lends a facile character to the public language of punishment and litigation is often at work. The abusive spouse or parent is likely to have been a victim of the same kind of abuse. In subtler but no less destructive ways, parents can model a corrosive approach to relationships that is first imitated and then transmitted from one generation to another. Economic and social privation can brutalize life in a broader way, creating an atmosphere of hopelessness that forces young adults to conclude that there is little or no hope that they can build lives marked by a measure of security and well-being.

This is not to say that there is no such thing as a wrong choice or sin. Nor am I suggesting that even people whose lives have been shaped by the settings in which they were raised and nurtured are without responsibility for the choices they make. But on closer examination, what seems to present itself as an example of explicable if not acceptable suffering is often far harder either to explain or to accept. As a result, even the public discourse about justice can become suspect, as the law and punishment are used to force an explanation of simple proportions on a loss with hidden complexities.

Acts of God

When we have finally traced the layered and hidden complexity of suffering, some of the most disturbing and unexplainable experiences are what, unfortunately, the insurance companies refer to as "acts of God." These are the mute, destructive forces of nature that God appears to control. Indiscriminate and uncontrolled, they often level the poorest communities, sweeping human life, the young and the old, ahead of power that we can do little or nothing to counter. The hurricane that swept Honduras, leaving Miguel's village and others buried in mud, is an example, but it is a single example of events that happen with such regularity that the net effect is almost numbing, including tornadoes, hurricanes, earthquakes, and drought. For example, by 2025 sub-Saharan nations will not be able to feed more than 40 percent of the one billion people who will live there. Due to declining soil fertility, forty-eight of those countries can only feed 70 percent of their populations now;[7] and famine already threatens the lives of 1.8 million of Somalia's 6 million people.[8] With good reason, one journalist describes Africa as "a battleground of contending dooms."[9]

Unseen Forces

As our knowledge of medical science grows, it is becoming clear there are still other, previously unseen forces deeply at work in shaping the character and suffering of our lives. Genetic research, for example, offers the promise of new treatments for disease. But it is also revealing the silent killers that claim the lives of millions. Codes at work in our own bodies set the stage for what research professor John Avise calls a "chromosomal house of horrors," including cystic fibrosis, Alzheimer's disease, type 1 breast cancer, and Down's syndrome.[10]

Even our knowledge of genetics may lead to new kinds of suffering. Researchers are already keenly aware of the potential conflict in families that knowledge of one family member's genetic makeup can cause. Parents who are silent carriers of a disease passed on to their children have to deal with feelings of guilt. Relatives of those who fall seriously ill from a genetic disease can suffer *Schadenfreude*, the shame-joy that comes with having escaped a fate that those who are close to them have not escaped. They can also experience anxiety about the possibility of contracting the diseases that others in their family already have.

Recently, however, a new threat has surfaced. The British government opted to give life insurance companies access to genetic information, revealing the identities of those who carry genetic markers for Huntington's disease, a crippling illness that almost inevitably leads to an early death. As a result, those who

already face the peril of a deadly disease may soon discover that
they are without insurance protection that will provide for their
families' needs.[11] They also face the possibility of being denied
employment.

A Family Resemblance

These experiences then, those that are individual and universal,
some marked by unacknowledged, layered, and hidden complexities, are the focus of our conversation. In discussing the problem
of suffering, I will rely more on stories than on definitions.

There is a place for a systematic attempt to define what we
mean when we talk about suffering. There are those, for example, who would distinguish the pain and struggle caused by the
process of maturation from the pain and struggle associated
with suffering. There are also legitimate questions associated
with the power and clarity of our perceptions. Just as there are
differences in our thresholds for pain, there are differences in
our perceptions of what constitutes suffering.

Whatever the value of those distinctions might be, here it is
enough to establish through the stories I am telling and the stories you might tell that the suffering which presses us most for
an explanation is suffering that bears a "family resemblance," a
body of common characteristics.[12] Without the benefit of a pre-
cise definition we can, nonetheless, recognize the loss and sense-
lessness that attends persistent suffering. "We know it when we
see it." It has no redemptive purpose; it cannot be described as
the equivalent of "growing pains." We experience its impact as
brute loss. It wreaks havoc that can be recognized across cultural and temporal boundaries; and even the philosophers who
struggle to define it resort to terms that echo the stories of pain
that are associated with it. The German philosopher G. W. F.
Hegel describes events of this kind as the "slaughterbench" of
history.[13] The English philosopher Alfred North Whitehead
describes it as "perpetual perishing."[14] But it amounts to much
the same. It is my story, yours, and ours.

CHAPTER TWO

Running the Risk of Conversation

Why We Need to Develop a Theology of Suffering

> *Faith and life negotiate. How right they should, if life is to be faithful and faith is to be alive.*
> —Kenneth Cragg[1]

To invite a conversation about the experience of suffering is an invitation to run certain risks. In a culture like ours, which is oriented to solutions and answers, a conversation about the why and wherefore of suffering is not likely to achieve the kind of closure that we instinctively require. There will be something provisional or incomplete about any answer we might give to the question "Why do we suffer?"

In addition, the answers we ourselves give to this question have been forged in the crucible of our own lives. As such, the thoughts we have on the subject are often hard-won and they are the means by which we have given meaning and significance to the suffering we have encountered. To discuss our suffering, then, is to invite conversation about something that is deeply personal, rooted in our understanding of both God and our life story. For that reason, the discussion can lead us to revisit deep losses.

It may also challenge the understandings that we forged along the way. Those understandings are rarely a matter of idle speculation. They can be the means by which we survive the suffering we experience; they may be the way in which we attribute meaning to our suffering; and they may be the means by which we continue to shape our lives in the wake of the suffering we experience. As a colleague of mine once observed, "Having relied deeply on some answers to survive that I can now no longer own, I am reticent to take away the 'crutches' someone uses before they are ready to move on."

These and probably other factors make it difficult to broach the subject of suffering and doubly difficult to broach the subject in a book. Nonetheless, I am convinced it is worth running the risk of that conversation. In what follows I invite you to consider the reasons I give for that exchange, not just as a justification for the conversation itself, but as a guide to some of what you might gain from it. By way of overview, then, my reasons are these. A conversation about suffering is:

- a necessary counterpoint to our culture of denial;
- an important exercise for people of faith;
- a means of negotiating the tensions between our experience of suffering and the assumptions we make about the way in which God works;
- a corrective to the logic of the health and wealth gospel;
- a means of nurturing emotional and physical well-being;
- a means of nurturing moral responsibility;
- a necessary resource, because we are all the authors of our own triage theology.

We will take each reason in turn.

Countering Our Culture of Denial

We have already touched on the universality of suffering. Suffering is, quite simply, something we all experience. Behind the closed doors, behind the apparent success and well-being of our neighbors and friends, lies the experience of suffering. Everyone has suffered, is suffering, or will suffer; and everyone knows someone who has, who is, or who will.

Nonetheless, we often deny its existence. This tendency is particularly common in today's world, where we are aware of tragedy not simply in the small communities of which we are a part, but in communities across the world as well. Modern technology has brought us closer together and it is now possible to follow the shape of a crisis in vivid detail. Unlike the more localized tragedies of which we were once aware, we are now alerted to events that we can do little or nothing to address. The steady flow of information we are provided feeds our anxiety and concern, but we find it difficult to identify ways to respond.

As a result, we look for ways to suppress the anxiety that the information creates. As Americans we are not unique in this regard, but we are particularly adept at this kind of denial. Advertising ploys crowd all but the youngest and strongest to the margins of our consciousness. Good looks and good fortune are promoted as an entitlement. We are inclined to talk about the lifestyle we *deserve*, the freedoms we have *earned*, and the comforts that *should* be ours; and we thereby weave a fabric of public discourse that suggests suffering is neither likely nor inevitable.

This cultural counterpoint has become such an important part of our psyche that we treat economic freedom and personal well-being as a near synonym for freedom itself. Saks Fifth Avenue invites us to "live a little"[2]; the city of Las Vegas advertises your right to "form your own party"[3]; and Salon Selectives invites you to "free yourself."[4] To some extent, of course, each is meant to be a play on words, a clever means of hooking people's attention. But our cultural conversation also betrays a deeper set of convictions. Much of the conversation in this country that revolved around the prospect of new-found freedom in the former Soviet Union focused on economic freedom and opportunity, not on responsibility.

Where the cultural counterpoint cannot completely compensate for our anxiety, we insulate ourselves, filtering the information we receive through a series of cultural lenses that are not unlike the personal lenses we use. The suffering that counts is the suffering that touches us most directly. I can still remember, for example, a network news program in which the crash of an Ethiopian airliner appeared third or fourth in a list of items, topped by fairly innocuous economic news from our own country. Everyone on board died; it is difficult to imagine that, if Americans had been involved, it would have been treated in the same fashion. More recently, *The New York Times* relegated the death of nine hundred people in West Bengal to a half column on page eleven in an edition dominated by the presidential campaign.[5]

In spite of what we might have expected, then, the media have not just brought us closer together. We have also used them to drive away anyone whose suffering does not personally touch us or (in the case of celebrities) enthrall us. The result is a world that feels less tangible, or deserving of our attention, than it should. This state of affairs is not simply an inevitable by-product of the technology itself. Travel to Europe for any length of time and you will discover countries that are not only physically closer, but are socially and psychologically closer to the average European in a way that the rest of the world is not close to many Americans.

Nor is this sifting of the world's suffering the only way in which we evade its suffering. Modern media are also the engine of escapist entertainment that further insulates us from the suffering around us. Movies and television have long functioned in this way. The content of both has hidden and trivialized the pain that we all experience, either by hiding human suffering completely or by exposing us to concentrations of violence that are spiritually numbing and are often treated as if they were of little or no consequence.

More recently video games, computers, and the worldwide web have added new layers of insulation from the suffering around us, but with significant differences. They have added exponentially to the amount of time we spend with such diversions. We now give our attention to more than one medium, and at times we give our attention to more than one medium at the same time! The media are now portable. So it is possible to unplug from the world around us in airports and on planes, as well as at home. And they now enlist our participation. While the media of television and movies expose us to numbing levels of violence, video games actually enlist us in perpetrating the violence.[6] Together, these strategies to evade the suffering around us help to create the impression that we can live without suffering. Indeed, we have so deeply appropriated this outlook that we often confront illness and death as if they are without precedent. At least as it applies to death, Woody Allen accurately captures the American mindset: "I'm not afraid of death, I just don't want to be there when it happens."[7]

But any experience that is so much a part of our world cries out for candor. We cannot ride the wave of denial that shapes our own culture's reaction, however comfortable that may be. It will not serve us well, nor is it easy to imagine a message worthy of being called "good news" need rely on that measure of insulation from the realities around us.

The Deeper Problem for People of Faith

For people of faith, the need to grapple with persistent suffering is particularly critical. For those who either believe that there is no God or believe that God is unconcerned with our well-being, suffering may bring both physical and emotional pain. But at a far more basic level the suffering can have a matter-of-fact character. There is little or no reason for an atheist to imagine a world without suffering, or to experience a world marked by suffering as somehow problematic or contradictory. But for people of faith there is a deeper problem. If, on any level, we believe that God is good or that God cares for us, then the presence of suffering is something that we may experience as radically contradictory. For that reason, suffering can be a source of existential anxiety and pain as well.

Broadly speaking, among people of faith there are two major divisions of opinion on approaches to the problem of suffering. One approach attempts to provide an explanation for its presence in our world, probing both experience and theology. Another approach, often called the faith solution, argues that even to attempt an explanation is, in and of itself, an act of faithlessness.

The latter is an understandable position. No response to the problem of suffering is likely to be complete. As theologian John Hick puts it, we can only hope for "less inadequate answers" to our questions.[8] The faith solution makes a virtue of the inevitable defects in those answers. By asserting there are reasons for our suffering that we cannot know, those who take this position offer the consolation that all of our experiences have an unknowable purpose. At the same time, they also avoid the burden of explanation and the risk of offering a less than perfect response.[9]

Any one of us who cares deeply about our faith has been tempted to adopt this approach. But sidestepping the questions that arise in the wake of our suffering is not an approach without serious problems. Anxious to vindicate God at any expense, the faith solution builds its case by suggesting that suffering, however devastating, is a blessing in disguise. Treating the whole of life as if it were Jimmy Stewart's *It's a Wonderful Life*, we are asked to suspend every power of judgment available to us, waiting for Clarence the angel to reveal all.

This is a particularly dangerous point of view when we take into consideration the suffering that we can either cause or prevent. To suggest that there is no explanation for suffering, or that by extension God is responsible for it, can foster and nurture fatalism. It encourages resignation to forces that are deemed to be beyond our control, undermining the will to act, to intervene, or to oppose injustice. It can also underwrite a lack of passion for social justice by painting the harsh realities around us as simply a part of God's plan.

Of course, there are those who would argue that the most basic value at stake here is that of reverence, or respect for God. Based on the conviction that everything that happens to us happens at God's bidding or with God's permission, some people will insist that anything we learn about the world must be made to fit with that conviction. To do anything else is at best irreverent and at worst heretical. For people who feel this way, any position that dwells at length on human suffering or underlines the destructive character of that suffering is likely to do God an injustice. Specifically, people who take this position fear that candor about the world around us will suggest either that God is not the one who causes everything to happen or that God is exceedingly cruel.

But how much of our theology is based on a reverent contemplation of our faith and how much of it is based on a candid assessment of the world around us will always be in question. To think theologically is, by definition, to contemplate the divine. For that reason, anything we say about God will always require a certain amount of humility and reverence. It would be arrogant or irreverent for us to claim we completely understand "the mind of God."

At the same time, however, the only language we can use about God is all too human, and because we are tied to this earth and the forces that shape it, our knowledge of God will always be provisional. But, to some extent, the genius of the Judeo-Christian tradition seems to lie in its willingness to think long and hard about the way in which God is at work in the world. Faith leads to candor, honesty about the way things are. We are freed to use our minds and our senses, to draw on our experience and the experience of others. Indeed, properly understood, faith should give us the confidence and courage to enter even more deeply into life's realities. Reason and experience are not infallible guides. They are flawed and fragmentary windows into the work of God in the world. But blind reverence is hardly an alternative. That is why even though the Christian tradition speaks of divine revelation, most Christians have also consciously granted that reason and experience also must be taken into account when we make theological statements.

To some extent, then, the choice between reverence and candor is not ours to make. The difference in the ways we choose to talk about suffering will always be that of balance. But, for a number of reasons, I am convinced that any theology of suffering that is likely to be of any value necessarily gives the candor of faith its due.

The candor of faith in the Judeo-Christian tradition has proven its value over the millennia. It is, for example, a hallmark of Old Testament theology. The psalms give free expression to candor, exploring in poetry and song the suffering that bedevils not only individuals, but the entire nation as well.

> My God, my God, why have you forsaken me?
>   Why are you so far from helping me
>   from the words of my groaning?
> O my God, I cry by day, but you do not answer;
>   and by night, but find no rest.
>   (Psalm 22:1–3)

Exposing the pain that people experience in wrenching detail, the psalms neither hide nor minimize the harm done. Instead, they reveal the immediate injury inflicted and the bitterness that follows.

> Save me, O God, for the waters have come up to my neck.
> I sink in deep mire, where there is no foothold;
> I have come into deep waters, and the flood sweeps over me.
> I am weary with my crying; my throat is parched.
> My eyes grow dim with waiting for my God.
>   (Psalm 69:1–3)

When pain and weariness gives way to vengeance, here again the psalmist is relentlessly candid.

> Let their table be a trap for them, a snare for their allies.
> Let their eyes be darkened so that they cannot see,
>   and make their loins tremble continually.
> Pour out your indignation upon them,

and let your burning anger overtake them.
May their camp be a desolation; let no one live in their tents.
    (Psalm 69:22–25)

The precedent for candor about the suffering we experience can also be found in the prophets. Reflecting the same commitment to candor, the prophet Habakkuk writes:

O LORD, how long shall I cry for help, and will you not listen?
Or cry to you "Violence!" and you will not save?
Why do you make me see wrongdoing and look at trouble?
Destruction and violence are before me; strife and
    contention arise.
So the law becomes slack and justice never prevails.
The wicked surround the righteous—
    therefore judgment comes forth perverted.
    (Habakkuk 1:2–4)

Writing in the late seventh century B.C.E., the prophet struggles with the disparity between the promises of God and the fortunes of his country, raising question after question without ever providing a sustained answer.

Are you not from of old, O LORD my God, my Holy One?
    You shall not die.
O LORD, you have marked them for judgment;
    and you, O Rock, have established them for punishment.
Your eyes are too pure to behold evil,
    and you cannot look on wrongdoing;
why do you look on the treacherous,
    and are silent when the wicked swallow
    those more righteous than they?
    (Habakkuk 1:12–13)

There are literary and historical reasons for the apparent imbalance between the number of questions that the prophet raises and the answers that he provides. The book may be the product of more than one prophet's work; the prophet's oracles may have been preserved piecemeal, and one or more oracles may have been lost. But whatever the reasons, the fact that the ancient Israelites so often preserved questions of this kind in both poetry and prophecy is, in and of itself, startling. In fact, to the modern mind the profoundly troubling questions the prophet asks may even appear misguided. Why ask questions you can't answer? Why burden the faithful with difficult questions? Why put God on the spot?

There was a time when I would have shared some of these misgivings about the place and function of the profoundly troubling questions that both the biblical prophets and poets ask. But with the passage of time I've grown to appreciate their willingness to ask them, because in so doing they accomplish three things. They give us permission to ask our own questions about suffering. They model the capacity to ask questions we might otherwise suppress, but can never escape. And they model how those questions might be asked without fear of compromising our relationship with God or with other people.

What is at stake, however, is not the modern preoccupation with the *right* to ask questions that arise out of a well-intentioned liberalism, or even a developmental perspective that embraces the *value* of asking them. Both of those preoccupations are shaped by our cultural struggle over asking questions, and they are the modern counterpoint to our fear of questions. By contrast, the poets and prophets of the Bible are interested in neither the value of questions, nor in the right to ask them. Instead, they are motivated by what the Jewish scholar Abraham Heschel describes as the motives or the passion of someone who is *homo sympathetikos*.

> The pathos of God is upon [the prophet]. It moves him. It breaks out in him like a storm in the soul, overwhelming his innerlife, his thoughts, feelings, wishes, and hopes. It takes possession of his heart and mind, giving him the

courage to act against the world. . . . The unique feature of [his] religious sympathy is not self-conquest, but self dedication; not the suppression of emotion, but its redirection; not silent subordination, but active co-operation with God; not love which aspires to the Being of God in Himself, but harmony of the soul with the concern of God.[10]

This is the context in which the prophets raise even the most pointed questions. Passionate to understand and confident that God is gracious, the prophets' search for answers is safeguarded by the very God whose behavior, at times, is in question. Straining and agonizing, they look for the hand of God; they are anxious to cooperate in God's work; and they are compelled to describe the way in which the nation can respond. So, the passion to ask questions and the willingness to be candid about the answers—or the absence of them—goes hand in hand with faith.

However, the relationship between questions, candor, and faith leaves the modern *homo sympathetikos* in a difficult position. The vast majority of the people around you resist the questions you will want to ask about the nature of suffering. Some of those who resist the questions are skeptical. There is too much suffering in the world and too much that counts against the existence of God to go on believing. So, the skeptics don't think you ought to believe and because they don't, they don't see the point in asking the questions. Others are certain God is in charge, and to ask questions is to display either a lack of confidence in God, or irreverence for God. They too don't think you should ask questions.

The first group would like to have proofs, but they are sure the proofs are unavailable. The second group is convinced we have the proof in hand, and so they believe. What neither group can admit is that they have more in common than they are prepared to acknowledge. Proof, or its absence, is so central to what they are prepared (or not prepared) to believe that neither group is willing to risk the pilgrimage of faith, or the life of a *homo sympathetikos!*

The approach that the poets and prophets of the Bible model corresponds to our experience and offers a way both to live in faith and to exercise candor. Both the questions and the confession of faith are there, as they should be. The prophets and poets strain and search for understanding and act on what they learn. But getting answers to their questions is not the basis of their relationship with God. "The righteous," Habakkuk observes, "live by their faith."[11]

Negotiating the Tensions between Experience and Faith

This is not to say that negotiating the tensions between what we believe and the suffering we experience is without importance— far from it, in fact. When, as people of faith, we address the tension between what we know from above (by means of revelation) and what we know from below (by means of our senses), it is necessary to make some kind of judgment about "the way we know what we know."

Some will argue that any and all knowledge of God is, by definition, revealed. A radical disjuncture between what we know about God and what we know about the world is, therefore, not particularly problematic. If what I know about the world somehow contradicts what I know about God, then I am either mistaken, or my knowledge is somehow incomplete. Revealed knowledge, as it were, trumps anything I might know by other means. Taking the most radical form of this position, there have been people who argued that everything to be known about God, if knowable at all, is known by exercising special powers of spiritual perception.

But another way of looking at this issue holds that because we and the world are God's creation, there is a certain amount of continuity and congruence between what we know about everyday affairs and what we know about God. This does not mean that there is no such thing as revealed truth, nor does it mean that our knowledge of either this world or God is not without defects or limitations. But it does mean that our knowledge of this world is relevant to our knowledge of God, and it does mean that we could be just as mistaken about what we take to be the revealed truth about God as we are mistaken about other matters.

The second of these positions is the one that, when brought to bear on the subject of suffering, forces us to acknowledge the reality of the loss and pain that people experience. It is not an easy position to take. And it lacks the dogmatic certainty of the faith position. But it is a place where the answers given, whatever their shortcomings, are more likely to acknowledge the realities of life as we experience them. For that reason it is also the place where our knowing from both above and below is most likely to offer us a unified and balanced way of knowing that engages both our experience of God and our experience of the world around us.

By contrast, the faith solution is bought with a price. The existence of suffering—its bald, almost incomprehensible character—takes us to the brink of unbelief in a way that almost no other experience can. Photographs of war, violence in our schools, and the aftermath of natural disasters lead us to doubt the goodness, if not the existence, of God. The faith solution holds all of that at bay, by denying the legitimacy of our experience. Insisting that our experience is unreliable at best, and a source of temptation to unbelief at worst, the faith solution denies us one means of knowing and understanding the suffering we experience.

A kind of spiritual schizophrenia results, forcing us to live in two worlds—one bounded by knowing from above and the other shaped by knowing from below. Functioning fully within the world with our senses while at work and play, we are forced to lurch from one way of knowing to another in times of crisis, abruptly setting aside our experience and turning instead to faith. The potential consequences are difficult to catalog and are not always predictable. But for some people they can be devastating, emotionally and spiritually.

By contrast, a faith that runs the risk of conversation can integrate the ways we understand the suffering that we experience, saving us from self-destructive denial. We are also likely to nurture a deeper faith in and dependence upon God. The ability to acknowledge the pain we experience prompts us to rely more immediately and deeply on God, negotiating from the beginning the tensions between what we experience and what we believe God's role may or may not be as it bears on our experience. We move closer to the truth and to God as a result, freeing ourselves from the need to protect our faith from a clear apprehension of what we experience on a day-to-day basis.

Correcting for the Logic of the "Health and Wealth Gospel"

An extreme expression of the faith solution is the "health and wealth gospel" that has emerged in some fundamentalist Protestant churches. Supported by a small circle of well-financed celebrities, ministers of the health and wealth gospel subscribe to the notion that healing and financial well-being are determined by the strength of our faith in general and the character of our prayers in particular.[12]

On one level, their enthusiasm for the logic of their position is understandable. Taken at face value, they are moved by a desire to teach people that their faith in God is well placed and that they should act on that faith. It is also not surprising that, in a world that struggles for meaning and purpose, people of faith attempt to give lived expression to their faith.

But on another level, to argue that this hard-and-fast, almost formulaic connection exists between our faith and our physical and financial fortunes is deeply problematic. As we will have an opportunity to explore at greater length in the next chapter, there is ample reason to believe that health and wealth preachers can only defend a connection of this kind by looking at life selectively. Were this no more than a purely academic question, the difficulties in a theology of this kind might not matter greatly. But the theology of the health and wealth gospel has a far wider impact.

In some cases, that impact is of an immediate and devastating nature. Urging his followers to refrain from calling a physician and to pray with faith, Hobart Freeman's directives led to the death of eighty of his followers from 1977 to 1984. By the time the press began to scrutinize the life of his community, the number of deaths in Freeman's community had risen to ninety a year.[13]

The impact of the health and wealth gospel extends beyond the immediate communities that its advocates lead, however. Years ago as graduate students, my wife and I lived across the street from Charles, a history professor, and his wife, Nancy, who taught handicapped children. Nancy, like so many women in our world, was the victim of breast cancer. Struck with the disease before greater emphasis was placed on early detection and before more effective treatments were discovered, she experienced a remission of the disease, but it was short-lived.

Throughout her battle with cancer, a fairly large circle of friends covenanted to pray for her on a regular basis. To their credit, they largely proved to be a community that was readily able to embrace her suffering. But when the cancer returned, one of the people in her circle of friends (not unlike some of those in Job's circle of friends!) let Nancy know that there must be someone in the group who was failing to pray with faith that she would recover, and that this probably accounted for the return of the disease. Wanting to be thorough, she also held out the possibility that it was Nancy herself who might lack the necessary faith.

Fortunately, Nancy was a woman of enormous emotional and spiritual maturity. For that reason, what could have been a second tragedy was hurtful, but it had little other impact on her overall well-being. There are, however, many people who experience an added dimension of guilt and fear as a result of theology of this kind. The incident also underlines the extent that the assumptions of the health and wealth gospel shape the faith of a far wider circle of people.

Far harder to track or describe is the impact such thinking has on the larger church's theology of suffering. Stripped of their ability to talk candidly about the experience of suffering without being treated as lacking faith, church members are forced to address the issue of suffering with a false optimism rather than Christian hope. Cure—temporary relief from an illness—is confused with healing—which brings with it inner elements as well as final deliverance from frailty.

Nurturing Emotional and Physical Well-Being

The perils associated with the health and wealth gospel are not the only ones our theology of suffering presents. Our understanding of suffering also has implications for our emotional and physical well-being in larger ways

Granger Westerberg, a Lutheran cleric and member of the University of Illinois Medical School in Chicago, notes that potentially as much as a third, or perhaps even two-thirds, of all illnesses occur at times of profound loss.[14] Whatever the actual figures may be, all of us know people who, in the wake of a traumatic experience, were "never the same again," or "died of a broken heart."

Not all of these experiences can be averted by giving careful thought to a theology of suffering. The origins of such experiences are far too complex and the nature of the grief we experience can be unrelated in critical ways to the theological assumptions we make about their experience. The nature of the loss we experience, our emotional makeup, the presence or absence of a support system, and the life story we bring to the experience all have a profound impact on our emotional and physical well-being. But a sense of isolation, added layers of guilt, and even a crisis of faith can arise under such circumstances, and there is little doubt that such struggles can either complicate or deepen the grief we encounter.

At least some of those struggles can arise out of the absence of opportunities to risk a conversation about the way we understand our suffering. When we are confined to the understanding we forge for ourselves, that understanding is marked by inevitable limitations. Those limits may be shaped by experience, by maturity, and by the specific nature of the loss we experience. But whatever the factors, the chance to candidly discuss our understanding can save unnecessary guilt or confusion before we enter the "eye of the storm."

Already convinced this was the case, I had its importance confirmed for me some years ago. Invited to speak to a parish over the space of six weeks about the subject of persistent suffering, I noticed that some of the most animated participants in the class were in their sixties and seventies. At the end of the six weeks a group of the older participants approached me. "We want to thank you," they said, "for giving us the opportunity to discuss these issues. We find ourselves at a new point in life. We are confronted in new ways with our own mortality and the mortality of those we love most. We have reluctantly said good-bye to parents, spouses, dear friends, and, in some cases, our children. Those experiences have raised new questions for us, but we've hesitated to say anything because the younger members of the church see us as completed human beings and paragons of faith. We haven't wanted to upset them or shake their confidence in God." Running the risk of conversation can create a space in which needs of this kind can be met.

Nurturing Moral Responsibility

Because we inflict suffering on one another, conversations about a theology of suffering can also serve as a means of nurturing moral responsibility. In complex ways, some theologies of suffering have, in the past, helped to preserve institutions that were the engine of suffering. Implying that things are the way they are because God wills them, the church has helped to reinforce abusive and oppressive structures that promote suffering. Theologies that preserve a destructive status quo, or that underwrite destructive practices as the will of God, can short-circuit the energy that might otherwise be devoted to the reduction of suffering. Working to reduce suffering can also sensitize us to the ways we inflict suffering on others.

Years ago I was asked by a Lutheran congregation to facilitate a series of conversations based on a booklet called "Scandals of the Faith." The subject matter was devoted to darker chapters in the history of the church. I can't remember now whether the authors actually gave attention to the deeper wellsprings of that history, but what each chapter clearly underlined was the profound connection between the church's theology and its moral failure. One section, for example, dealt at length with the way the church countenanced slavery. Approving the sale of husband and wife to different owners, ministers then moralized with the slaves themselves about the sin of adultery inherent in marrying someone else living on the same plantation.

The lesson should not be lost on us, but we repeat the same mistake over and over. When we fail to candidly discuss the suffering we inflict on one another, we can fail to recognize the suffering at all; we can compound the injury we do to one another; and we cut the nerve of moral engagement that can stimulate us to take action.

A Resource for Triage Theologians

Expanding, then, on the observations that I made at the beginning of this chapter and naming them in a slightly different way, we need to recognize that we are all triage theologians. Moving through life, we assess our needs, define our relationship to God, and shape our understanding of how God intersects with our lives. We are like an emergency room physician, performing a triage or assessment of a patient's condition. We measure the significance of our suffering, describe the meaning we find in it, and gradually fashion a theology that in turn shapes our lives.

My wife Elaine and I have often referred to May of 1978 as "the month from hell." I was looking forward to graduation from seminary and the chance to "turn the tables." For the first time I was going to have an opportunity to teach and Elaine was midway through her master's and was teaching full time. In spite of the rites of passage that lay ahead, however, it had been a difficult year.

My father-in-law had battled bone cancer for two years and the illness was making devastating progress. The doctors were obviously groping in the dark, trying chemotherapy regimens that were increasingly experimental in nature—all of little value. Elaine and I lived near Lexington, Kentucky, at the time, and we made trips to Detroit as often as possible, putting thousands of miles on a car that traveled few other distances in the space of a year. Leaving late Friday afternoon, we drove straight through, stopping only to refuel the car.

Living so far away, there was little that we could do to help on a regular basis, but on the weekends we weighed in to do what we could. Dad had been seriously weakened by the treatments he was receiving and could no longer get out of bed on his own. To make matters worse, he was so restless that he and my mother-in-law could no longer share the same room. So they pinned a bell to the mattress that allowed him to signal for help.

He was forced to rise three or four times a night, so during our visits I assumed my mother-in-law's responsibility for getting him out of bed. He was often unable to get back to sleep and we had a number of mid-night conversations. By the end of the weekend I was usually exhausted and wondered how my in-laws were able to survive from week to week.

With everyone's attention focused on my father-in-law's health, Elaine's grandfather died suddenly of a stroke. Although in his nineties, he had enjoyed phenomenally good health, but in a week's time he was gone. Seventeen days later, long before anyone seriously expected it, my father-in-law died as well.

On the way out of his hospital room I ran into one of Elaine's aunts, who made a well-intended remark that betrayed a strange set of assumptions: "Well, I guess God was lonely and now he has Joe with him."

Much of what is said in times of grief possesses the same ragged edges and unexamined assumptions. Searching for comfort and meaning, we "try on" ways of explaining our loss and testing our perceptions in conversation with one another and ourselves. Some of what is said is of only passing significance, part of an emotional triage that moves us from place to place. Assessing injury after injury like a physician in an emergency room, we abandon some of the views we express almost immediately, knowing that the diagnosis is either untrustworthy or of little or no help to us. We live with other explanations a little longer, finding them helpful but only for a period of time, and still other parts of that process lodge in our hearts and minds, becoming a part of the story we tell to explain our experience.

Over time, a kind of informal or personal theology emerges. It may not be cast in one-word labels or in the technical jargon that a professional theologian uses, and we might not even recognize it as "theology" in so many words. Instead, we might use a phrase, a sentence, or a story and gradually build on them. But whatever we say, the views we express function in much the same way as a theology does, shaping our view of God, life, and its purpose.

This personal triage theology represents a spiritual force that shapes the minds and hearts of millions and, truth be told, shapes the thinking not only of lay people, but of "religious professionals" as well. Indeed, because it is a part of that deeply personal triage, it might be argued that this theology is of greater significance in most of our lives than are many, if not most, formal theologies.

In spite of the importance of the triage theology, we rarely discuss our views in a reflective or critical fashion. Knowing the deeply personal and often painful origins of those beliefs, we fear that any criticism we might make of someone else's views will appear uncharitable, if not cruel. That fear is not without reason. Years ago, as I began discussing the subject of suffering, a young couple became extremely agitated and asked me a number of pointed questions. It was only later that I learned they had encountered problems with infertility that made it impossible for them to conceive a child. In the process of "doing" their own triage, they had concluded this was God's way of leading them into a life of caring for foster children. Convinced that their infertility was God's will, they were unable to achieve any emotional distance from their own experience. As a result, they interpreted my remarks on the subject as an attack on their faith and, in a sense, as a criticism of their lives.

It is this very dynamic that helps to explain why so few tough-minded comparisons are made between views of suffering. People may be prepared to question others on almost any subject, but to question someone's interpretation of the events in their lives that have caused them to struggle and grieve is easily seen as an attack on that person.

Nonetheless, I am going to run the risk. I ask you to separate the ideas from the people, and I will do the same. I invite you to do this for a number of reasons. First, care and concern are misplaced when they conspire to silence critical thinking on a subject such as suffering. Suffering is so complex and so devastating that it demands more, not less, of the critical attention and thought that we give to other life experiences. It may be excruciating to even have the conversation, but the need for a conversation outweighs the pain involved.

Second, there has been so much said on the subject of suffering that an exercise in "ground clearing" is extremely helpful. In some ways, I think it will be easier for you to understand what I can affirm and easier for you to decide what you can affirm if I begin by outlining some of the answers I have found troubling or unsatisfactory.

Third, when attempting to allow an answer to "grow in us," it is as important to recognize the limitations of some answers to our questions as it is to discover better answers. All too often the personal theologies we fashion and share with others are narrowly addressed to our own experience, without giving due attention to the larger realities of human experience; or they are offered in defense of a particular understanding of God.

We declare our deliverance to be an answer to prayer, but we do not take into consideration the experience of someone who prays without the same results. We talk about God's using a particular experience in our lives after the suffering has passed, never acknowledging the way in which those "lessons" are completely obscured by the grief or pain someone else continues to suffer.

I am convinced that this tendency grows partly out of the process of triage itself. We naturally work through possible answers to our own questions, and the relief that comes from having found an answer that meets our needs often prompts us to offer the same solution to others. I am also convinced, however, that we tend to rely on narrowly personal answers to the problem of suffering because of the increasingly privatized character of our faith. The "priesthood of all believers" having run amok, we have failed to realize that there is a difference between thinking theologically for ourselves and thinking theologically only about ourselves. The former has to do with our responsibility as people of faith; the latter is dramatically limited in what it can offer. Unable to embrace the experience of others, it may not even serve to accurately describe our own experience. The discoveries we make in reflecting on the shape of our own lives need to be tested against something larger, including the experience of others.

CHAPTER THREE

Cold Comfort

Answers That Might Work, but Probably Don't

> *I could not understand why Nacino, who did good in trying to help*
> *Ultima, had lost his life; and why Tenorio, who was evil and had*
> *taken a life, was free and unpunished. It didn't seem fair. I thought*
> *a great deal about God and why he let such things happen. When*
> *the weather was warmer I sometimes paused beneath the juniper*
> *tree and looked at the stained ground. Then my mind wandered*
> *and my thoughts became a living part of me. Perhaps, I thought,*
> *God had not seen the murder take place, and that is why He had*
> *not punished Tenorio. Perhaps God was too busy in heaven to*
> *worry or care about us.*
> —Rudolfo Anaya[1]

Because we draw so narrowly on our own experience in shaping
a theology of suffering, some of the explanations we try on
along the way can be of cold comfort to others. They can also
seemingly serve us well at one point in life and completely fail
us later at another, leaving us to wonder whether our faith in
God was ever justified. On such occasions we can see such
experiences as a "no" to continued faith, or we can see them as
an invitation to re-examine the shape of our faith.

Here, then, are some of the explanations I have either set
aside, or believe are of limited value. I have been drawn to some
of them in the past and some of them I have mistrusted from
the moment I heard them. You will probably have had much

the same reaction. There are undoubtedly others that could have been listed here. But these explanations appear more often in the personal triage theologies I have heard along the way. They also represent many others that appear in slightly similar language, but are much alike in content.

I also have chosen to describe them using the language of the triage theology that we all have had to shape somewhere along the way in our lives.[2] The invitation is to explore your own theology of suffering; to test its value in describing the larger human experience; and to begin forging a theology that can more accurately capture not only your experience, but that of others. It is a process that requires a certain amount of quiet deliberation and self-examination. It is also a process that may require exchanging old comforts for new ones.

We Suffer Because We Sin.

It is not unusual to hear someone suggest that persistent suffering is due to sin. The explanation is as old as—and probably older than—the Book of Job, and appears on the lips of Eliphaz the Temanite, one of Job's "comforters."

> Think now, who that was innocent ever perished?
>   Or where were the upright cut off?
> As I have seen, those who plow iniquity and sow trouble
>   reap the same.
> By the breath of God they perish,
>   and by the blast of his anger they are consumed.
>   (Job 4:7–9)

But we need not look that far afield for other examples. Bishop David Jenkins of England was repeatedly told that the lightning that struck the cathedral he served in York in 1984 was a direct result of the theological positions that he assumed.[3] Evangelist and one-time presidential candidate Pat Robertson argues that the Supreme Court's decisions on compulsory school prayer and issues of a similar nature brought "the wrath of God" down on the United States. As a result, he notes, we have suffered a series of tragedies, including "the assassination of John F. Kennedy, the 1969 stock market plunge, the rise in oil prices and U.S. trade deficit of the early 1970s, President Nixon's resignation, [and] the Iranian Hostage crisis."[4]

Both statements are representative of a common line of reasoning, but they usually rely heavily on a selective description of the actual events or on a far more narrow reading of history. David Jenkins's daughter told the reporters who cited her father's theology as the cause of the fire in York that if God sought to punish her father, then God is a bad shot. Her father happened to be in London on the day the cathedral was struck. Nor are Robertson's examples particularly persuasive. As journalist Bruce Bower observes, "American history before 1963 was at least equally crowded with unfortunate events; but Robertson counts on the fact that his readers, by and large, will not realize that. He also counts on his followers' image of the Almighty being close enough to his own that they will believe God induced Lee Harvey Oswald to kill Kennedy in order to punish the nation."[5]

There are, however, just enough examples to cite of a more direct and apparently simple nature that many people continue to argue that suffering is the result of sin. People will refer, for example, to the alcoholic whose addiction destroys his liver, the drug addict whose habit leads to an overdose, or the criminal whose behavior leads to incarceration. Suffering, in this reading of things, is a consequence of sinful behavior. The connection is simple, clean, and easily explained.

Couched in familiar theological categories, this view of suffering lends a reliable, even predictable, character to human life. In the face of persistent suffering, to argue that sin is the cause offers an explanation that can lend meaning to experiences that appear to be without meaning. It suggests patterns where there seem to be no patterns and gives a reassuring sense of justice to a world where there seems to be no justice.

God's role is not at all in doubt; God's immediacy is felt; and human life is worked out in the context of ever-present, divine judgment. The world of sin and its obvious consequences is one in which there is a place for everything and everything is in its place. The linear character of the explanation itself not only helps to account for suffering, but also serves to bolster faith in God and to provide a motive for the ethical demands one might make in the name of the gospel.

However, one of the greatest problems with even these apparently obvious examples is that here, too, the explanation is too simple. To begin with, the impact of suffering precipitated by sin is rarely confined to the life of the sinner. Instead, it has an impact on others. Both the alcoholic and the addict often have partners or children who suffer as well. For them, there are immediate implications. Their lives can be drawn into the orbit of codependency. They can become the victims of violence and abusive behavior, or they can lose a secure environment in which to live and grow.

A family's larger, long-term well-being can also be jeopardized. In order to achieve a healthy approach to building relationships with spouses and employers, the adult children of alcoholics are often forced to negotiate questions of self-worth and boundaries over an extended period of time. For some, the experience becomes a defining moment, reshaping whole futures.

Nor are the families of alcoholics the only ones affected. The victims of drunk drivers can be injured or killed, and the wider relationships of an alcoholic can be marred by abusive and destructive behavior. The victim, in other words, is not necessarily the sinner.

Even in the case of the sinners, the role of choice is often a murky business at best. Educators and psychologists have debated for some time now the question of how much of our behavior can be attributed to nature—our genetic makeup—and how much should be attributed to nurture—the way we are socialized by our families and by the societies in which we live. And that debate is likely to continue for some time to come. But no one who drives through the inner cities of America with their eyes wide open can fail to see why despair and frustration haunt many young urban children. As the campaign ad for one organization that I served helped to remind us, "You can't pull yourself up by your own bootstraps if you don't have a pair of boots."

Of course, this is only one example of the way in which the apparently simple connection between sin and its consequences is not as simple as it may seem. Children of divorced parents are more likely to be divorced and children who are abused are more likely to be abusive as adults. Grinding poverty is not the only engine of crime, failed relationships, or addictive behavior.

Factor in the genetic causes that may be at work, and the tendency to attribute persistent suffering to sinful behavior gives rise to a series of questions that are not easily answered. If genetics makes one person more susceptible to alcoholism than another, what then are we arguing? Is God in part the architect of the sins that condemn us to suffering? Is the inborn tendency itself a cruel test of some kind?

In addition to personal sins, other sins have a corporate or social dimension that can affect even larger numbers of innocent bystanders. The tide of racism, for example, has swept entire populations into slavery and concentration camps, ruining millions of lives and ending millions of others. In notable cases in our own century, the sinners have even escaped the consequences of their sin. Racially motivated murders committed in the United States during the sixties went unsolved, and one can only assume that the guilty succeeded in evading the consequences of their cruelty (at least in this life!).

From 1958 to 1964, one hundred thousand Romanians perished in forced labor camps because they were used to build the fifty-mile-long Black Sea Canal. They were imprisoned for their political views or because they belonged to the lower rungs of the economic ladder. But the architect of the scheme was sheltered by the former communist leadership of the Romanian regime. As a result, the very question of his responsibility was not even raised until he was eighty-seven years old.

Entrenched differences in the Middle East continue to take lives of men, women, and children. Some die as a result of terrorism, others in the wake of disproportionate force exercised by the military. The loss of life is embedded in a long history of bitterness and acrimony, dispossession and fear; and the cycle of violence and inequity is sustained by political structures on both the Israeli and Palestinian sides that are deeply invested in the maintenance of political power. In all three cases the connection between sinner and suffering is not at all obvious.

This realization, of course, brings us face-to-face with an even greater complexity than the social dimensions of sin: the impact of sin on the victim. As Korean-American theologian Andrew Sung Park observes, Christians in the West have, more often than not, underlined the role and subsequent needs of the sinner in not only committing sin, but in suffering its consequences. As a result, we are accustomed to speaking of repentance, forgiveness, and redemption, all of which focus on the sinner.[6] But one of the issues that the moralistic focus on sin-as-an-explanation-for-suffering leaves unexplained is the suffering incurred by the victim. In this case the simple equation of action and consequence fails completely.

Finally, none of this bears in any direct way on the suffering caused by natural catastrophes, disease, or even errors in human judgment. Unless you talk in terms of some kind of "cosmic dislocation" caused by sin (a thought we will return to in chapter five), we can all think of cases in which suffering has been precipitated by events that are without any explicit moral significance. Earthquakes and pilot error, even well-intended choices with unintended consequences, have all played a part in the landscape of human misfortune. Some of these causes of human suffering are, quite clearly, driven by considerations that have nothing to do with human behavior: the faults in the earth's crust that are specific to a particular part of the world; the weather patterns around the globe; the progress of disease.

Other causes of suffering, although brought about by human action, are hardly a matter of moral choice. Pilot error, a design flaw in a cable car, and the failed maintenance of railway lines illustrate our fallibility, but not our sinfulness.

Far too much suffering, then, cannot be explained by simply citing sin. Too much of it is senseless, brute loss with no one to blame. Too much of it is visited on life's little sinners, while the big sinners go free. Too much of it is caused by errors in judgment, or by a tragic mixture of other factors that are not, by definition, sin; and the simple connection between choice and consequence is often absent or obscure.

Suffering Is God's Will.

One of the long-standing explanations given for suffering is the one that argues that everything—good, bad, and indifferent—is the will of God. Part of its apparent strength is its simplicity. The possible explanations for suffering are to be found in the shape of our conduct before God. Part of this view's emotional appeal is that it promises a certain kind of unshakable consolation. No matter what happens to us, it is God's will. Borrowing on the logic of the faith-solution we discussed above, it is also the kind of explanation that makes a deceptively strong claim to "orthodoxy" by refusing to question anything that might happen to us.

The emotional power of this view is difficult to overestimate. I have known people experiencing unimaginable suffering who have embraced this reassurance, as well as people who have argued that God visits the greatest suffering on those he loves and trusts most. For a time, at any rate, it was also the explanation that consoled a Vietnam veteran I know who was made a quadriplegic by a sniper's bullet just days after getting married. The conviction that all suffering is God's will is a particularly important reassurance for those who believe strongly in the sovereignty of God as the power to control all that happens in the world.

For all its apparent strengths, however, this approach is fraught with numerous difficulties. Pastor and writer Leslie Weatherhead underlined one of those difficulties in a series of sermons he preached at City Temple in London during World War II. Recounting time that he had spent in India, he found himself attempting to comfort a friend as they stood on the veranda of his home. Weatherhead's friend, John, had lost his son to a cholera epidemic. Beside himself, the man paced the veranda while his daughter, who had survived the epidemic, was sleeping in a cot covered with mosquito netting at one end of the porch.

Finally, in despair, John turned to Weatherhead and declared, "Well, padre, it is the will of God. That's all there is to it. It is the will of God."

Weatherhead shocked his friend by asking, "Supposing someone crept up the steps onto the veranda tonight, while you all slept, and deliberately put a wad of cotton soaked in cholera germ culture over your little girl's mouth as she lay in that cot there on the veranda, what would you think about that?"

Almost offended by what he believed was an obvious, if not cruel question, John responded, "My God . . . what would I think about that? Nobody would do such a damnable thing. If he attempted it and I caught him, I would kill him with as little compunction as I would a snake, and throw him over the veranda. What do you mean by suggesting such a thing?"

"But, John," Weatherhead responded, "isn't that just what you have accused God of doing when you said it was his will? Call your little boy's death the result of mass ignorance, call it mass folly, call it mass sin, if you like, call it bad drains or communal carelessness, but don't call it the will of God." Weatherhead concludes, "Surely we cannot identify as the will of God something for which a man would be locked up in jail, or put in a criminal lunatic asylum."[7]

In other words, as comforting as this view is, it leaves us with a God who is both cruel and criminal. A few people feel honorbound to hold that this might actually be the case. Reading the

Bible in both literal and historical terms, they point to the Book of Job, noting that God gives the devil permission to wreak havoc with Job's life. There are many things that might be said about this approach to the Bible and to the Book of Job itself. Not every image of God that appears in the biblical text, for example, can be easily accommodated, if we are bound to build our view of God in equal parts out of every description the Bible gives. Where, for example, are we to put the image of God as one who is prepared to call for child sacrifice, even by way of testing the faithful, as in the case of the sacrifice of Isaac (Genesis 22:1–14)? And just because the psalmist prays for the death of his enemies' children, does that mean that God entertains prayers of this kind (Psalm 21:10; cf. 37:28; 109:12–15)?

But an added difficulty in reading the Book of Job in this fashion is that the book itself is probably not historical at all, and the celestial scene at the beginning of the book is certainly not historical. So, far from having morning coffee with Satan on a regular basis and giving him permission to torment this and that human being, God does not function in this way. Nor do we need to accommodate the picture as a part of our view of God. Instead, the conversation between God and Satan is a dramatic setting designed to let the reader know that, contrary to his friends' views (which are described later in the speeches of Job's comforters), Job is not suffering because he is guilty of some sin.

Of course, the vast majority of people who hold the view that God permits suffering to happen do not believe that God is either cruel or criminal. They typically believe that God has a hidden purpose, or they exempt God from the moral values that govern mere mortals.

The latter, it seems to me, is completely untenable. Theology, in a sense, takes its lead from the character of God. If God's character is simply a mirror image of human character, then, as Dorothy Sayers observes, God is a bully, only larger and more arbitrary.[8] We are left without a starting point for our understanding of God that rises above even base human behavior, and while that is not out of the realm of possibility, a God fraught with human frailties is not likely to serve as either the object of devotion or the means of our salvation. In fact, the fortunes of that kind of God are likely to be much like the fortunes of the gods of the Greek pantheon, and in a day of TV soap operas, the entertainment value in a God of that kind is limited. We have other means of exploring human depravity!

Nor does the notion that God has a hidden purpose completely escape the same criticism. The argument that a larger design is in the making when there is suffering overlooks the fact that the individual events include actions that are themselves often immoral or evil. So, for example, if a wife or husband is betrayed by a spouse, something positive may emerge, but the action of betrayal is still what it is, a betrayal. So, anyone who is prepared to argue for a greater design is forced to also argue that God prompts people to do evil.

In more morally neutral territory, where the causes of suffering are natural forces or accidents, the notion that certain events are blessings in disguise is easier to maintain, but only if you limit the number of examples you use. An isolated misfortune may yield great empathy and acts of kindness, or it may lead to an unexpected goal. Deafness may seemingly contribute to the genius of a Beethoven. But other events overwhelm the victims, and as the number of examples grows, it becomes more difficult to sustain the argument that a tapestry is emerging. The argument can only be defended selectively. Apply it more generally and it collapses under its own weight.

Some people might die full of years, but many are killed and injured early in life. Some people may survive the evil done by others, but some do not and the evil done is evil nonetheless. And whatever good may emerge over time, tragic, senseless waste and loss happen over and over again. Our inability to acknowledge that reality is neither necessary nor characteristic of the Judeo-Christian faith, but lies instead with a latent fear that to acknowledge the reality of waste and loss is somehow to surrender the possibility of faith. We so completely identify the notion of sovereignty with God, and the exercise of power with the notion of sovereignty, that to acknowledge its existence is to vanquish God from heaven.

It is a tendency that has more in common with the residual rationalism of our own culture than with the heritage of our faith. The only God worth having, from our culture's point of view, is a God who is what we would like God to be—in control. By contrast, the Judeo-Christian tradition at its best always has acknowledged the reality of evil and the tragedy in life. Those experiences may have raised questions for the prophets or prompted poets to write psalms lamenting a loss, but neither the experience nor an honest acknowledgment of our grief is ever seen as fatal to our faith. Instead, both the Jewish and Christian traditions have, in somewhat different ways, celebrated the conviction that God is present with us in the midst of our suffering.

God Uses Suffering to Teach Us.

A closely related approach to the problem of persistent suffering is the argument that God uses suffering to teach us. It ventures beyond the bald assertion of God's control to suggest that the purpose is often, if not always, to teach us something. In this way, so the reasoning goes, the things that happen in our lives are not nearly as important as the transcendent lessons to be learned. Knowing this better than we do, God uses, even orchestrates, the suffering we experience to teach us those lessons. The challenge is to discover the lesson to be learned and embrace it without reservation. Those who turn their backs on those lessons are, by definition, unteachable.

There can be little doubt that we "learn" from suffering, and herein lies the power of this explanation. Suffering radically simplifies life, alerting us to the ways we have given priority to more trivial considerations and have failed to focus on the more important aspects of life. It prompt us to re-examine the shape of our faith, our use of time, the attention we give to relationships, and the freedom we possess to live courageously.

This happens in large part because suffering has a way of cutting through the pretensions and pettiness that so easily assert an influence on our lives. Over time we easily lose touch with the larger, lasting values that should shape our choices and we are, instead, drawn steadily and irresistibly into ways of living that are shaped by a succession of seemingly less significant decisions. This is why, in a certain sense, every generation has to rediscover truths that, on the face of it, might appear to be lessons that we could collectively learn and capture for the entire human race.

It is in moments of suffering that we discover just how distorted our lives have become and often, though not always, people who have suffered are also people of profound substance. This is, perhaps in part, because the experience of suffering has pushed them to re-evaluate their lives in radical ways.

But there is a critical difference between suggesting that the human spirit can learn from suffering, and suggesting that God sends suffering our way in order to teach us even the most important of life's lessons. The first point of view has no immediate bearing on the role played by God, unless it is the work of the Spirit in the victim's life. The second point of view suggests that God's role is active and calculating.

Our ability to accept the second view relies again, as it did above, on our tendency to suspend our capacity for moral judgment, exempting God from the same criteria we bring to bear on our own lives. The only difference between the sadistic God of Weatherhead's story told above, and this God, is that the latter is also a teacher, who is a sadist.

I am a father and at one stage it was very important to teach my daughter something about the inherent dangers of touching the burner on a stove and of crossing the street. The best possible instruction I could give her was preventative in nature. Carefully, clearly, and with a sense of urgency, her mother and

I helped Lindsay to understand the consequences of touching a stove and of crossing the road without looking left and right. This is exactly what any caring, thoughtful parent would do. If, however, we had taught her the same lessons by allowing her to touch an open flame, or cross a street unassisted, Child Protective Services would have had every reason to take her from our custody. It was reasonable for us to teach her those urgent lessons. It would have been cruel to use pain and danger to bring those lessons home, no matter how well she might have learned them. And yet, here again, without reservation we attribute the same kind of cruelty to God. The logic can neither give us a God worthy of our love, nor comfort those who suffer.

We Suffer Because We Don't Pray or Don't Have Faith in God.

In her book *God's Will Is Prosperity,* Gloria Copeland describes 3 John:1–2 as the biblical basis for one of what she describes as "the laws of prosperity." The Elder writes: "The elder to the beloved Gaius, whom I love in truth. Beloved, I pray that all may go well with you and that you may be in good health, just as it is well with your soul." Copeland concludes: "You will prosper [materially] to the degree that your soul prospers."[9]

For many of us, our understanding of suffering is closely tied to the strength of our faith and, more specifically, our confidence in Scripture. For that reason one way of understanding passages from the Bible on the subjects of suffering and well-being can loom large. According to that understanding of Scripture, our strength of faith is intimately tied to our well-being. So the argument goes, if we are unwilling to pray or if we pray with a lack of faith, then God will not intervene in our lives and we will suffer as a result.

For some of us, this conviction can take on an almost formulaic character, in which we use a series of steps to focus our efforts to pray with faith. Evangelist Kenneth Hagin responds to that need and the Gospel of Mark in this way. Recalling an experience in prayer that he had in December of 1953, Hagin describes an encounter with God:

> I said, "Dear Lord, I have two sermons I preach concerning the woman who touched Your clothes and was healed when You were on earth. I received both of these sermons by inspiration. I preach them everywhere I go and every time I preach them, I seem to be conscious in my spirit that the Holy Spirit is trying to get another sermon from this fifth chapter of Mark to me—a sermon that would complement the first two. . . . If I am right about this, I wish You would give me that sermon."[10]

In the sermon that follows, Hagin treats the elements of the story as if they were the steps in a formula for achieving prosperity. Hagin declares, "You can write your own ticket with God." Like the woman in the story, who first declared her faith before she touched Jesus, "Say it," Hagin urges. "Positive or negative, God will give to you according to the desires you express." That's step one. Step two: "do it." Like the woman in Mark's story, "Your action defeats you or puts you over." She felt that her body had been healed. Step three: "receive it." "Faith is the plug," declares Hagin. "Just plug in." When Jesus asked who had touched him, she admitted that she had in the presence of onlookers. Step four: "tell it."[11]

Thinking of this kind is not at all uncommon in our culture. In fact, it is so common to find this point of view in some circles that journalists have dubbed the beliefs expressed by Hagin and Copeland as the health and wealth gospel, underlining the connection between faith, well-being, and freedom or deliverance from suffering. For those who have entertained this way of viewing the persistence of suffering, the ability to move outside of this way of thinking and believing is enormously difficult. To rethink the health and wealth gospel is by definition to lack faith, and the persistence of any suffering that we experience simply becomes confirmation that we do not believe, as we should, in the power of prayer. Because this line of reasoning is so often derived from Scripture, many Christians also struggle with the added anxiety that to rethink their understanding of Scripture is a demonstration of their lack of confidence in God's word and promises.

For that reason it is important to realize, however, that this approach to reading Scripture is not the only approach, but is actually problematic. Take, for example, the opening line of 3 John mentioned above: "Beloved, I pray that all may go well with you and that you may be in good health, just as it is well with your soul." This might be read as a promise, but the verse is actually taken from the opening line of a letter. In fact, it comes from one of the New Testament's few pieces of private correspondence, and it begins precisely where you and I would begin, with a fairly typical well-wish for good health, extended to the letter's recipient. As a result, to read the passage as if it were a promise or even a spiritual principle is actually to mis-read the letter's intention. John the Elder's well-wish is just that, a well-wish. It is doubtful that he believed even the material prosperity of Gaius was guaranteed, let alone that of succeeding generations of believers.

In a similar fashion, reading a story from the Gospel of Mark as if it were the record of four steps to prosperity is also problematic. Handling the text in this fashion, there is little that any composition cannot be made to say. If we are genuinely interested in the message of the biblical text, then our approach to the text must be governed by the conventions of the literary genre that the writer chooses to use. Judged against that standard, it is clear that the Gospel writers were not trying to outline a formula for healing.

The descriptions in Mark's Gospel are used to move the action along, to introduce the characters in the narrative and the thoughts that occupy their minds. Narratives should not be atomized. The story has a certain impressionistic or cumulative character; the message is understood only when read as a whole. In short, to read Mark's Gospel in this fashion is to treat the story as if it were a cookbook or a do-it-yourself manual.

Given the shape of the gospel narrative, it is also strange to assume that the essence of the gospel can be reduced to the achievement of health and wealth. Jesus ministered to the poor and suffering. He identified care for the poor as a direct measure of the love that people have for God. He suggested that the kingdom, rightly understood, reversed the fortunes of rich and poor. And he identified "the least of these" as the pre-eminent citizens of that kingdom.

But, he did not make deliverance from poverty or suffering the goal of his ministry. Instead, he seems to have treated the miraculous as a sign of the kingdom's presence, and even then he discouraged those who followed him from publicizing those events.[12] To the extent that he talked about suffering on behalf of the kingdom, he appears to have argued that his followers could expect suffering to be the hallmark of discipleship.[13] It is difficult to understand, then, how suffering can be described as evidence of a lack of faith.

The problems we face in thinking this way about our suffering are not problematic simply in terms of the way we read the Bible. The problems are also profoundly theological in nature. To argue that the persistence of our suffering is the measure of our faith gives greater weight to the relationship than the larger biblical message actually warrants. The mechanistic, if not magical, view of both God and prayer implied in this approach is equally alien to the Christian tradition. Reduced to something like a cosmic Coke machine that, if manipulated, will respond to our coaxing, God does little more than dispense elements of the American dream; and prayer is little more than a matter of getting the formula right.

Worst of all, perhaps, it is a view that implies that the incomprehensible suffering that whole nations experience is simply a matter of failing to get the formula right. If it is true, as I suggested in chapter one, that our own experience is an inadequate window into the dynamics of suffering, then there is another problem with tying the strength of our faith to the persistence of suffering. And the problem is this: In a country that enjoys the level of general economic well-being that we do, it is possible to sustain the health and wealth line of reasoning with some success, simply by virtue of our well-being. At least some of us will experience fewer illnesses, live longer, and be able to insulate ourselves from some losses, relying in large part on our own wealth and the benefits of the collective wealth we enjoy. But that option is scarcely possible elsewhere in the world.

Far too many people across the rest of the world live their lives at or below the poverty line to entertain a theology of this kind; and in many cases the socioeconomic structures that shape life in those societies render any kind of significant change difficult, if not impossible. The caste system in India, the established social roles of women in many societies, the widespread economic difficulties in the former Soviet Union, and the permanent underclass in our own cities are all examples of systemic factors of this kind. Their experience, no less than ours, should give us pause.

God Doesn't Will Us to Suffer, but Allows Us to Suffer.

Of all the explanations for evil and persistent suffering, the view I have been most attracted to in the past is the view that distinguishes between God's willing certain events to happen and God's allowing them to happen. Developed in Leslie Weatherhead's sermons written during the London Blitz and in the triage theology of many other people, this approach seemingly moves beyond the notion that God wills suffering to happen.[14] Arguing that God intended one fate for humankind at creation and now adjusts our fates to our sinfulness, this view holds that God *allows* suffering to happen. Taking refuge in this shift in language, it is more palatable because it appears to remove God from an active role and because it traces the suffering to our collective and individual sinfulness. It is also intellectually more attractive in that it avoids more obvious forms of divine sovereignty that simply assert that God causes everything to happen. Ultimately, Weatherhead and others argue, God will reassert his will, realizing his intention for the whole created order.

But is there a real difference between God actively willing disaster and God permitting it to take place? I am not convinced there is. Returning to the illustration I gave above, if my child is about to touch a hot stove or cross the street without assistance and I can stop her but choose not to intervene, at the very least wouldn't I be guilty of negligence? And if God is an all-knowing parent, doesn't this apply in an even more severe way to God? And why does the random and sometimes destructive suffering that occurs impact the innocent and weak? In the final analysis, there seems to be very little difference between the act of permitting suffering and willing it that is not semantic.

The Shape of Our Thinking

This list of cold comforts could be extended almost endlessly. As I discussed my thoughts with a friend and colleague some years ago, she observed that the cold comfort she had been offered was the reassurance that God intended to bless others through her suffering. At first, she observed, this argument had a certain appeal. It gave meaning and purpose to an otherwise meaningless, grinding struggle; and she admitted that the notion of being used by God in this way appealed to her ego, giving her a special place in God's economy. It is a variation on one or more of the views I have already described, and is problematic for some of the same reasons.

A pattern emerges, however. The explanations given vary only in two ways. One variation revolves around the question of how immediately God is involved in precipitating the suffering that happens in our lives. For some, God is the cause or architect of our suffering, shaping both the timing and the shape of the experience. According to others, God acts less immediately, permitting suffering to take place.

As already noted, the difference is largely semantic. But in the triage theology that each of us fashions, the distinction suggests a difference that is critical to many, suggesting that God is more directly involved or less directly involved in shaping the suffering we experience. Differences in emphasis exist, of course, but the explanations lie along a spectrum, each of which emphasizes that God is or exercises power.

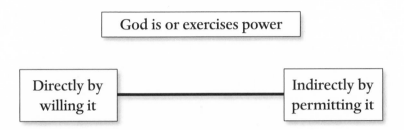

God is or exercises power

| **Directly by willing it** | | **Indirectly by permitting it** |

The second variation revolves around the motives that each person either attributes to God or believes we can know. For some, the critical information revolves around knowing why God brings suffering into our lives. Whether God seeks a greater good or hopes to teach us something, motive looms large. For people who stress those motives, knowing why God causes us to suffer can be all-important, justifying what seems to be without justification. For those who embrace the faith-solution, the task of providing a motive is, as we have said, set aside.

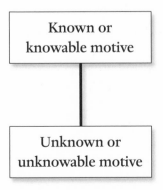

Known or knowable motive

| **Unknown or unknowable motive** |

Nonetheless, even those who adhere to the faith-solution insist on the active or permissive role of God in bringing about the suffering that occurs.

Together the cold comforts described form a grid of sorts along which might be placed the answers to the problem of suffering, characterizing both the measure of God's active engagement in the experience of suffering and our knowledge of God's motive.

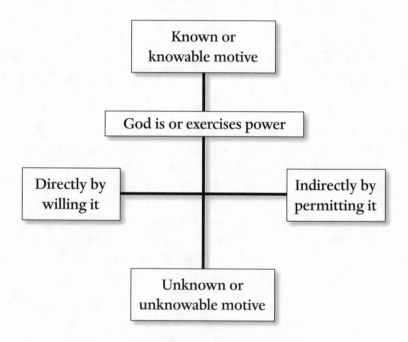

Presumably the only variable is the way our role is said to influence the behavior of God.

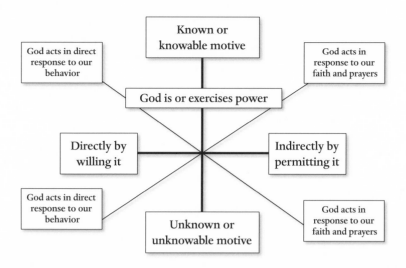

Completed, the major axes of the grid reflect the focus of most responses to the experience of suffering, centering on God as actor and initiator or, in the case of Weatherhead's view, gatekeeper. Central, too, is the question of whether God acts in this capacity with a motive or without a motive and, secondarily, with reference to our actions as a dimension of that motive or without such reference. Just why these concerns chart so much of what is said in our triage theologies, and just why the power or sovereignty of God figures so prominently in them, is, in large part, the subject of the next chapter.

CHAPTER FOUR

God Is Great, God Is Good

The Origins of Cold Comfort

God is great, God is good, let us thank him for our food.

Far from approaching the problem of suffering anew, we grapple with our experience of pain and loss against the backdrop of accumulated assumptions and beliefs. Specific notions about God, or what psychologists call "God images," play a particularly important role. These images determine the role we assume God plays in shaping the suffering we experience. They determine the degree to which we expect God to be actively or passively involved. They can be the basis on which we attribute certain motives to God for causing us to suffer, if we believe that God does; and they can shape the extent to which we expect God to deliver us. If the suffering we experience poses a problem for us, the way we define the problem also may lie in the assumptions that we make about God.

The Origin of God Images

In some cases the God images we use are part of the triage theology that arises out of our experiences. Our view of God can be shaped, for example, by the images of care and nurture that we transfer to God from the experience of being parented. If we are treated in warm and loving ways, one set of images has a chance of dominating. God will be the parent who cares, the mother or father who nurtures, protects, and guides. If we are denied that warmth and love, other images may prevail. We may think of God as punitive or cruel, scarcely aware of or moved by our pain. The latter may even render the notion of God unthinkable.

Formative experiences, including injuries and loss, can also shape our views of God in decisive ways. Based on those experiences and the extent to which we struggle with them as people of faith, we may draw any number of conclusions. We may conclude that God cares about us and intervenes in our lives on a regular basis. We may decide that God does intervene, but not in a predictable fashion. Or we may feel that God has little or no immediate interest in our needs at all. Still other influences on the shape of the God images we use include the larger circle of people we know and trust. Teachers, religious leaders, mentors, and significant peers can have a decisive impact on the shape of our thinking.

As this last example suggests, however, not all of the vocabulary that we use to describe God will be shaped by our personal experiences or by purely personal categories. Shared assumptions that grow out of a common religious, cultural, or intellectual environment can have a profound impact on the way we image God. So, too, can race and social setting. Some of those influences and the impact they have can be readily identified. We can, for example, point to images from Scripture and tradition or from worship and song that from an early age have shaped the way we think about God.

Still other influences, however, are barely visible to us. Like stones dropped into a pool of water that cause a series of ripples on the surface of a pond, they continue to shape the way we think, having an impact that lasts for centuries in some cases. But the stones—the influences themselves—drift to the bottom, hidden from view.

We don't live for centuries, of course, but the influence of a particular way of thinking about God can live on in a creed, in hymnody, or in the teaching of a significant church leader. In fact, God images of this kind cannot only remain influential, but gain power and apparent legitimacy by being preserved in this way. And, if images of this kind become a part of institutional practice or tradition, their power can endure for centuries. Generation after generation can be introduced to those images as a "given" of the faith, a matter of orthodox belief, a conviction to be defended.

If these influences on the way we think about God were either completely benign or a matter of idle speculation, it might not be particularly important for the vast majority of people to give them much thought. But because our God images tend to shape the way we think about our life and faith, such images are filled with the potential for defining the way we experience the world. In particular, the way we think about God as it applies to the subject of suffering can be a source of grief or encouragement, despair or hope, confusion or clarity.

God as Power, God as Good

In the case of suffering, there is no more influential pair of God images than the twin assumptions that God is both powerful and good. Cited over and over by those who debate the problem of suffering, the two images are thought of as reasonable and in sharp tension with one another. Writing in the eighteenth century, the English philosopher David Hume put the problem this way:

> Is he [God] willing to prevent evil, but not able? then is he impotent. Is he able, but not willing? then is he malevolent. Is he both able and willing? whence then is evil?[1]

Hume was an atheist. So at first one might wonder whether Hume puts the problem in this way in order to make a case against the existence of God. But closer attention to the history of the debate clearly demonstrates that he is hardly the only one to put the problem this way.

The same assumptions about God also figure in the description given the problem by the twentieth-century Christian apologist C. S. Lewis:

> If God were good, He would wish to make His creatures perfectly happy and if God were almighty He would be able to do what He wished. But the creatures are not happy. Therefore, God lacks either goodness or power, or both.[2]

Strikingly, the problem is the same for both Hume and Lewis, as well as for many others. We assume God is powerful. We assume God is good. But the fact that we suffer and the way we suffer seem to make one of those two assumptions impossible to defend. So in coming to terms with the problem of suffering, we must think carefully about both images.

We will find that, in thinking about those images, at least part of the reason it is so difficult for us to acknowledge the gravity of our suffering *and* live as people of faith lies in the assumptions we make about God. Tracking the "stones" dropped into the intellectual and theological water in which we live, how did we get here?

God and Power

The notion that God is power or one who wields power is not a novel concept. Probably human beings always have grappled with this notion in one way or another. The ancient Greeks, for example, often attributed much of what happened to them to a capricious exercise of power by their gods.

In Christian and contemporary contexts, however, the notion of God as power or as one who wields power is an image that can be traced to at least three formative influences that continue to shape the way we image God. One is the emphasis that natural theology places on what is called the "argument from design." A second is the emphasis that the Protestant Reformation places on the sovereignty of God. The third is the tendency of both ancient and modern believers to think in magical categories.

Each influence is important because it has contributed to a distinctive way of thinking about God and has, in turn, shaped our thinking, even though we may not use the same words. The argument from design emphasizes God's role as powerful creator. The Reformation emphasis on divine sovereignty emphasizes God's role as the author of personal destiny. And the magical categories that have never completely disappeared from Christian theology treat God as power to be manipulated. As different as each image is, all three reinforce the notion that God is power or one who wields power. Let's look at each one in order.

God as creator

Part of the emphasis placed on divine power in conversations about the problem of suffering began with the human fascination over the apparently orderly and interdependent nature of the world in which we live. This interest is not new, nor is it a distinctively Christian interest. The search for an explanation that can account for the complex patterns that govern our world and the larger universe is at least as old as recorded history and probably older. The ancient Greeks were fascinated with those patterns and with the quest for an explanation for their existence. But the idea that the ordered character of the world is the work of a divine creator using a design or plan is the product of Christian reflection on the subject. The great thirteenth-century theologian, Thomas Aquinas, went so far as to argue that the planets and stars were arranged by God to "obtain the best result."[3]

In making this "argument from design" for the existence of God, Aquinas was relying on what scholars call "natural theology." Simply put, natural theology moves from observations concerning the natural order to observations about the existence

and nature of God. Unlike "revealed theology," which ultimately relies on an encounter with God, natural theology
attempts to rely heavily or completely on the shape of the
world and the universe around us in order to make statements
about the divine. For example, Aquinas and others detect a
design in the eye's capacity for seeing and the ear's capacity for
hearing, and from that they posit the existence of God and
God's power to bring about that design.

Natural theology is a common endeavor and not without
merit.[4] Linking our knowledge of God with the knowledge we
accumulate from our senses can inform the theological statements we make. The conclusions we reach about God that are
derived from an encounter that might take place while reading,
in prayer, or while grappling with the traditions of the church
can also be compared with what we know on the basis of reason. There is a great deal to be said for a theology that is ham-
mered out in conversation with the world as it is. A theology
that is radically out of touch with the "real world" (which is,
after all, God's world) is likely to prove unsatisfactory, if not
unworkable. For example, any description of God's role in the
creation of the earth needs to be informed by an understanding
of our planet's history as informed by a study of geology,
physics, and the earth's origins.

For all its merits, however, natural theology has also created
considerable problems for a discussion of suffering. The feature
of natural theology that is most at fault is the language about
God that surfaces and surfaces forcibly. Again, look at the language used by Aquinas:

> We see that things which lack knowledge, such as natu-
> ral bodies, act for an end, and this is evident from their
> acting always, or nearly always, in the same way, so as to
> obtain the best result. Hence it is plain that they achieve
> their end, not fortuitously, but designedly. Now whatever
> lacks knowledge cannot move towards an end, unless it

be directed by some being endowed with knowledge and intelligence; as the arrow is directed by the archer. Therefore some intelligent being exists by whom all natural things are directed to their end; and this being we call God.[5]

Similarly, in what is widely regarded as the most famous statement of natural theology, Anglican priest and philosopher William Paley wrote in 1802:

[W]hen we come to inspect the watch, we perceive . . . that its several parts are framed and put together for a purpose, e.g. that they are so formed and adjusted as to produce motion, and that motion so regulated as to point out the hour of the day; that if the different parts had been differently shaped from what they are, or placed after any other manner or in any other order than that in which they were placed, either no motion at all would have been carried on in the machine, or none which would have answered the use that is now served by it . . . the inference we think is inevitable, that the watch must have had a maker—that there must have existed, at some time and at some place or other, an artificer or artificers who formed it for the purpose which we find it actually to answer, who comprehended its construction and designed its use.[6]

Outside the church, deists (people who believe that there is a God, but that God is not actively involved in human history) also argued that God is evident in the shape of creation. Physicist and mathematician Sir Isaac Newton said,

This most beautiful system of the sun, planets and comets, could only proceed from the counsel and dominion of an intelligent and powerful Being.[7]

In a similar vein, chemist Robert Boyle observed:

> The *excellent contrivance* of that great system of the
> world, and especially the curious fabric of the bodies of
> the animals and the uses of their sensories and other
> parts, have been made the great motives that in all ages
> and nations induced philosophers to acknowledge a
> Deity as the author of these admirable structures.[8]

It is immediately clear that the language used in a theology
of this kind stresses God's role as creative engineer and
designer, as one who exercises power and control. Now, given
the fact that a great deal of natural theology is focused on the
effort to confirm the existence of God, there is nothing particularly surprising about this emphasis. Relying on the argument
from design, natural theologians are, by definition, attracted to
patterns that suggest the existence of God, the presence of
divine activity, and evidence of God's creative role. For that reason, natural theologians are inevitably preoccupied with the
exercise of divine power.

But by the time God has been defined decisively as one who
exercises power and control, it is almost impossible to say anything more about God that does not somehow first accommodate this all-important definition. For example, a theologian
may assert that God grants us freedom of choice, but the same
theologian is often unwilling to grant that we can exercise those
choices in a way that raises any serious question about the
power of God. Or we may argue that Jesus faced temptation,
but we often go on to argue that Jesus could not have surrendered to the temptations he faced.

To complicate matters further, historically theologians and
believers have moved freely from natural theology to a revealed
theology, little realizing that in moving from the one to the
other they have embraced a very different way of talking
about God. Natural theology gives precedence to arguments
from design in large part because it relies on our powers of

observation and the clues available to us in nature. By contrast, the larger task of theology gives precedence to sources that make a very different kind of description possible, including a characterization of God that attempts to be more specific and draws on a history of relationships with the people of God tied to particular encounters.

Natural theology is not incompatible with this larger task. In fact, as I suggested above, it is worth articulating how natural and revealed theology can be creatively integrated. Natural theology is limited in what it can say about God; and revealed theology can be dangerously abstract if it is unrelated to the world as it is.[9] But because the two approaches rely on very different means of making statements about God, they do have distinctly different goals and they follow very different rules in formulating theological statements. Natural theology, because it confines itself to our powers of observation, can appeal only to the data available from patterns, trends, and features of the world around us, while revealed theology might cite the biblical text or the traditions of the church in attempting to describe God and the way God works in the world. Stories of the community of faith, what it learns from life's pilgrimage, and what it claims to discover in prayer are all potentially the raw material of a revealed theology.

In failing to give attention to those differences, the priorities of the one endeavor are overwhelmed by the priorities of the other. Aquinas's work is a good example. Without attention to the differences between the two approaches, he imports the priorities of natural theology, compromising what might be said from the vantage point of revealed theology. An emphasis on the power of God has to be accommodated again and again, particularly when dealing with the problem of suffering.

It would be a mistake, however, to assume that the emphasis on divine power can be laid at the doorstep of natural theology alone or that the people I've identified above were the only people to rely on natural theology. Protestant reformers Martin Luther and John Calvin both acknowledged that a certain amount could be known about God from nature, and both cited the power of God as one of the things that could be inferred about God from what we can see.

So, for example, Luther rejects the emphasis that Aquinas and others place on natural revelation, arguing that reason can provide only a "superficial" understanding of God.[10] He even argues that there is a gulf "between nature and grace, between reason and revelation" that cannot be bridged.[11] But he then contends there is a general revelation given to all human beings that permits them to know that there is not only a God, but also a God who is all-powerful (omnipotent) and all-knowing (omniscient). Only by "extinguish[ing] the light in [our] hearts" can we fail to be aware of this.[12]

In other words, Luther's quarrel with natural theology does not revolve around the issue of divine power. It revolves around how much can be known without revealed theology. For both Aquinas and Luther the earth is "wisely governed."[13]

A generation later, Calvin makes a similar case, but does so in a more direct fashion. Referring to the "book of nature" as a complement to Scripture, he argues that a study of the stars "unfolds the admirable wisdom of God."[14] What may be learned is of no saving significance. We cannot be redeemed through that knowledge, nor can we find forgiveness for our sins. But we can know that God exists and, as the creation demonstrates, we can gather that God is powerful.[15]

There is, then, no substantial difference between the views of either reformer and their theological predecessors.[16] The God of natural power makes a strong showing in the theological outlook of Catholic, Protestant, and deist—physicist, priest, and theologian.

God as author of personal destiny

If anything, however, the manifestation of God as power is strengthened in the theology of the Protestant Reformation. That makes it even more difficult to address the problem of suffering without first reckoning with a God who is—or should be—completely in control. This is the case largely because both

Luther and Calvin also assert that God is the author of our personal destinies.

In Luther's case, this development is embedded in part in his own triage theology and the formative experiences that shaped his own thinking. Describing the occasion of Luther's first celebration of the mass, Yale historian Roland Bainton recounts that the date originally set for the celebration was postponed for a month so that Martin's father Hans could attend.

Father and son had been alienated for years over Martin's decision to enter the priesthood. Hans had wanted Martin to become a lawyer, thinking that his son could support his parents in their old age. Martin's decision to enter the priesthood had introduced so much tension to their relationship that the two had not spoken to one another since the younger Luther had left home to attend university.

For that reason, the plan to celebrate his first mass with his father in attendance raised Martin's hopes that they could reconcile their differences. The day of the celebration Hans arrived at the monastery with his entourage and made a generous contribution to the monks' work. The occasion was off to a good start.

When Luther took his place behind the altar, however, he was haunted by a long-standing sense of unworthiness that, judging from the account, was deeply embedded in his relationship with his father. As he began to recite the introductory lines of the mass, he came to the words "We offer unto thee, the living, the true, the eternal God." At that point, Luther writes,

> I was utterly stupefied and terror-stricken. I thought to myself, "With what tongue shall I address such Majesty? . . . And shall I, a miserable little pygmy, say, 'I want this, I ask for that'? For I am dust and ashes and full of sin and I am speaking to the living eternal and true God.'"

Struggling to hold his emotions in check until he could finish the mass, Luther left the altar completely exhausted, and went to join his father and the other monks for a meal.

Looking for reassurance from his father, Martin said to Hans, "Dear Father, why were you so contrary to my becoming a monk? And perhaps you are not quite satisfied even now. The life is so quiet and godly."

But Martin received no words of reassurance in return. Instead his father exploded and, turning on his son in the presence of everyone assembled, shouted, "You learned scholar, have you never read in the Bible that you should honor your father and your mother? And here you have left me and your dear mother to look after ourselves in our old age."

Martin attempted to respond, arguing that God had called him to the priesthood in a voice from a thundercloud. But Hans was unmoved. "God grant," said Hans, "it was not an apparition of the Devil."[17]

"And shall I, a miserable little pygmy, say, 'I want this, I ask for that'? For I am dust and ashes and full of sin and I am speaking to the living eternal and true God.'" Luther's theology is rooted in his struggle with a profound sense of unworthiness, and his personal quest for some measure of relief was further frustrated by his experience of the church. His quest for meaning, then, drove him well beyond questions dealing with the created order and focused in particular on the fate of the individual.

In attempting to account for the destiny of his own soul and that of others, Luther concluded that salvation is, from start to finish, the work of God. To be sure, it was Luther's study of the biblical text that led him to this conclusion, but it was also informed by his desire to find a means of salvation that addressed the guilt he felt without relying on the practices of the church he felt had failed him. Accordingly, Luther was prepared to accept the notion that salvation is not only God's work, but that to accomplish that work God predestined all human beings to either heaven or hell.

Calvin made much the same argument and reacted to a somewhat similar mix of personal experience and his reading of Scripture. On the face of it, his work is far more systematic in character and marked by a considerable degree of apparent detachment. Certainly, it is fair to say that the tenor of Luther's work is marked by a far greater degree of passion and self-revelation than is Calvin's.

But behind the language of Calvin's work is a man whose theology reflects the anxieties of his contemporaries. Convinced that moral decline was overwhelming society, Calvin relied heavily on the language of "order and disorder, purity and contamination." He believed that not only the individual but the whole of society was threatened by this malaise,[18] and took comfort in knowing that God predetermined the shape of each individual's temporal and eternal destiny, dictating their life's work[19] and the course of human events.[20] History, Calvin wrote, illustrates

> how God has exercised vengeance on all those who devote themselves to cruelty, to rapine, and to other extortions; and next how he has punished lecheries and other infections when they have flourished too much; and then how he has punished perjuries; and that he has not been able to endure the pride of men. When we consider all that, should it not serve us well also today? Let us remember well this lesson, that since, from the creation of the world, God has not ceased to warn us that he is judge of the world, we should learn to fear him, and to walk carefully, and that the punishments that he has inflicted on the wicked should be to us so many mirrors and so many bridles to restrain us.[21]

Indeed, according to Calvin, God's control over history is complete and it is a mistake to look anywhere else for an explanation. "Whenever any adversity occurs . . . its causes are sought in the world, so that almost nobody considers the hand that strikes. When the year's harvest is bad, we consult astrology and attribute it to the conjunction of the stars."[22] Instead, he urges, we should "turn our minds to God and acknowledge him as the judge who summons us, as the accused, before his tribunal."[23]

For both Luther and Calvin, the sweep of God's power is far more particular than the picture we get from even natural theology. The God image at work in their theologies is more than the creator of the natural order. God is also the author of personal destiny, determining what we do, sending fortune and misfortune, heaven and hell.

These two traditions have heavily colored the God images we have inherited with notions of power. Because Aquinas, Luther, and Calvin have played such central roles in shaping both Catholic and Protestant thought, their influence has been considerable. But these influences are relatively easy to identify by comparison with the almost subterranean influence that magic has had on the Christian tradition.

God as power to be manipulated

The task of distinguishing magic from religion is a difficult one.[24] It is further complicated by the fact that what is magic for one person is often someone else's religion.[25] This has led scholars to test the use of a variety of criteria for making a distinction between the two. Others have surrendered the attempt to distinguish them, preferring instead to talk about a distinction between rationality and ritual instead of religion and magic.[26]

But this much is clear: when religion shades off into magic, God either wields power or is power; and ritual becomes a matter of manipulating, channeling, or tapping into that power. It is this way of viewing God that is, at least in part, the essence of magic.[27]

To many, the notion that magic has had any kind of influence on the church will seem an almost outrageous idea. But in fact, the history of magic's influence on Christianity is a long one, interwoven in subtle and not-so-subtle ways with the mainstream of Christian theology, worship, and practice. There are notorious examples from the Middle Ages, for example. Latin prayers were said in prescribed ways as a cure for disease; words penned on a piece of paper were worn around the neck;

burning or burying an animal alive was used to promote recovery; and mirrors or crystal balls were used to identify the kind of witchcraft at work in promoting an illness. Christians practiced so much magic, in fact, that clergy specifically challenged its use. In 1552 Hugh Latimer, bishop of Worcester, complained, "A great many of us . . . when we be in trouble or sickness, or lose anything, we run hither and thither to witches, or sorcerers, whom we call wise men . . . seeking aid and comfort at their hands."[28]

If magic were either a thing of the past or the eccentric preoccupation of a few people, then it might have little or no bearing on the God images that shape our thinking about the problem of suffering. But dependence on magic is hardly characteristic of the Middle Ages alone. Magical assumptions about God persist both inside and outside the church.

We have already touched on one such example in discussing the health and wealth gospel. The mechanistic character of that outlook, its emphasis on using the right words and on following the right steps, reflects a magical attitude toward God as a power to be manipulated. Set aside your crutches, make a positive confession, take the following steps—these and other practices reflect a notion of God as power to be accessed. There are both religious leaders and parachurch organizations whose ministries are based on assumptions of this kind, and there are many people who, at one time or another, think of God in this way. But the picture of God as a power that can be tapped in this way is not confined to the health and wealth gospel alone.

America's self-help culture today also exhibits a tendency to use magic to manipulate the world. Mixing religion, magic, and an occasional scientific insight, more and more Americans are applying an eclectic mix of mantras, prayers, and drumming in order to address illness and loss.

One man, for example, recounts a story of being alienated from a relative over religious beliefs. After a particularly unpleasant argument, he began suffering from a series of violent headaches. According to his account, the man tapped into the power of God by imagining a telegraph wire leading from himself to the offended family member, flooding the imaginary wire with messages of universal love.[29] www.newprayer.com promises to send the prayers of its customers to "God's last known location, the star system M13 where NASA locates the Big Bang," as if pinpointing God were like tapping into an appropriate place in a power source.[30] Still other, much older traditions of magical cures, continue to reject medical treatment in favor of relying entirely on the ministry of God. So, for example, people refuse to see a physician, cease taking their medication, or discard braces and crutches in a kind of public enactment of their dependence on God. As diverse as these approaches are, the consistent feature in all of them is the treatment of God as a power to be manipulated. In turn, this assumption shapes the way we relate to God in times of suffering.

The reasons for our fascination with magical approaches to God are neither difficult to identify, nor are they are unrelated to the factors that shaped the convictions of our medieval forebears. The people of medieval Europe grappled with unseen killers and death on an unimaginable scale as the bubonic plague moved across the continent. In 1563 the plague claimed the lives of twenty thousand people in London alone. It is not at all difficult to imagine why they lashed out in a variety of directions, looking for an explanation and a remedy, turning to charms and incantations, witches and spells. Although more than one factor accounts for the whole of magic's attraction, anthropologist Bronislaw Malinowski is right. Magic derives (at least in part) "from emotional responses to situations of frustration" and "impasse."[31]

By contrast, today we have pushed back the frontiers of ignorance and we have named the causes of death-dealing diseases, storms, and earthquakes. But it would be arrogant in the extreme to claim that we are immune to the same need for control over the world around us. Frustration and impasse simply appear in different places for us.

As a result, even the technology we have used to address the causes of pain and suffering has assumed a magical aura; and in turn magic has found a means of expressing itself through technology. Both trends demonstrate just how fragile the boundaries are between our own cultures and those of the past. Writers wax eloquent on the "divinity present in the digital." Biotechnology promises utopian visions of health. Longevity and the values of "quantity, speed, and growth" shape our worldview.[32] Threaded through our magazines and newspapers are utopian visions of endlessly expanding life expectancy and the conquest of disease.

Not surprisingly, in spite of our much-vaunted technological progress, we still experience suffering as impasse and frustration. The very fact that suffering still occurs is an occasion for dismay; and in those moments when we are overwhelmed by suffering, we (no less than those before us) are tempted to look for a magical deliverance. When we do, more often than not, the image of God as power takes center stage. As God has already secured a place in our vocabulary by both natural theology and the Reformation, we simply extend the God image in new directions.

The Goodness of God

The other God image that figures prominently in conversations about the experience of suffering is the goodness of God. The concepts of "the good" and of God as good are rooted in both ancient and medieval thought.

In ancient Greek philosophy, conversations about "the good" revolved at first around the question of ethics. Plato and Aristotle both discussed what a person might do that would achieve a good result. They discussed the good as both a virtue and as a goal, and they discussed the nature of the "highest good" one might achieve. The third-century philosopher Plotinus took this quest a step further and searched for a unifying principle that might epitomize the "Supreme Good." Building on the work of Plotinus, St. Augustine, the bishop of Hippo from 356 to 430 C.E., identified the Supreme Good with the God of Christianity, arguing that God represents perfection in "measure, form, and order."[33]

In turn, Augustine's work set the stage for Anselm of Canterbury, who lived from 1033 to 1109 and was the founder of the philosophical movement called Scholasticism. A monk and later Archbishop of Canterbury, Anselm sought a single argument to prove that God exists and has certain characteristics. Almost failing in the effort, he finally hit on the strategy of moving from the notion of God to the existence of God. By contrast with natural theology (which reasons from nature to God) and revealed theology (which reasons from an encounter with God to God), one might say that Anselm reasoned from the idea of God to the reality of God. Reasoning that the idea itself would need to allow for the infinity of God and a measure of perfection that was unsurpassed by anything known to humanity, Anselm began with the idea that the concept of God is the greatest idea of which one can conceive.[34]

To Anselm's way of thinking, this idea allowed for a concept of God greater than we in our own finitude can ever grasp and, at the same time, allowed for an understanding of God that transcended any and every other created being or force. On that basis, he went on to describe in detail the attributes of God, including (among others) omniscience, omnipotence, and goodness. Because he begins with the idea of God, Anselm describes that goodness in largely abstract terms, focusing on both the nature and morality of God.

Anselm's views did not win universal approval. Some preferred a different definition of God's goodness, emphasizing ethical or aesthetic categories. Others argued that his effort was misguided. It simply did not follow that the thought of God meant that God necessarily existed. In fact, if a show of hands could be taken among history's philosophers, the vast majority would probably dissent from Anselm's views.

But he shared enough in common with both St. Augustine (who preceded him) and the great medieval theologian Thomas Aquinas (who followed him) that his ideas became the storm center of an argument about the existence and nature of God that has raged on ever since. As a result, even those who differed with Anselm found themselves grappling with his approach and language; and, in turn, language about the goodness of God gained widespread currency. When the issue of suffering arises, then, philosophers on both sides of the question tend to take the goodness of God as a given in the debate, whether they think that suffering counts for or against the existence of a good God.

Of course, for most of us, the questions raised by Anselm are rarely the subject of conversation. But the notion of God's goodness is, thanks to Anselm, one of those unseen stones dropped into our religious and intellectual waters. We continue to feel the impact without necessarily seeing the stone itself. The ripples move across our intellectual and cultural waters, leaving us with the language of the philosophers even if we do not use their definitions.

The goodness of God as the capacity to care

Beyond the philosophical conversation about the goodness of God is a second, broader conversation in which we are all engaged. That conversation is devoted to the same subject, even though we might use our own definitions for the goodness of God instead of those used by philosophers and theologians.

Often our definition is, on the surface, fairly simple. God is good—or is not—because what happens in the world does—or does not—conform to our understanding of right and wrong, just and unjust. Not unlike Plato and Aristotle, we intuitively look at the world through ethical lenses; and, not unlike Augustine, we identify God as the embodiment of what we take to be the "Supreme Good."

When the events of life run counter to our sense of what is ethically good—the just suffer, or the unjust go unpunished—we look for an explanation. In response, some of us will argue that most or all of the suffering in the world can be traced to human, not divine, behavior. Others will excuse God from the ethical demands to which we ourselves feel bound, arguing the rules don't apply to God in the same way. Still others will argue that a greater good is at stake when suffering persists and that God is using the experience to accomplish that greater good.

For others, however, God is good because God cares for us. We measure the goodness of God against the barometer of human experience, the absence or presence of pain, gain and loss, joy and grief. Given our modern American cultural orientation, this definition of divine goodness seems to dominate.

Since we are bent on our own autonomy and well-being, the measure of God's capacity for goodness is given expression in God's capacity to care. At our best, we would like to think that God is good enough to protect us. At our worst, we think of God as the cosmic custodian of an existence that we work to achieve, labor to maintain, and fight to protect. God is often cast in the role of caring for those factors beyond our control. If Anselm's understanding of divine goodness was abstract in nature, our understanding of the same concept can be highly personal, and at times, even materialistic.

When Candor Comes

Of course, for both the philosopher and the layperson the goodness of God can be as nonnegotiable as the concept of God as power. For that reason, we find ourselves in much the same position as those who have gone before us—struggling to defend both assumptions about God, grappling with the same way of seeing the problem. How often have we prayed, "God is great, God is good, let us thank him for our food"?

In our effort to defend the God images on which we so deeply depend, we are tempted to explain away the suffering of others—to look for a blessing in disguise, a lesson to be learned. We are less candid with ourselves and, painfully, less candid with those who look to us for encouragement. And, if we fail to find a hidden blessing or a lesson to be learned, then all too often we urge one another to pray for a magical deliverance we cannot have. We find ourselves not only believing that God *can* be moved by magic, but that we *ought* to believe that God can be moved by magic. When, at long last, the reality of the pain and loss that accompanies suffering is admitted—when we are candid—then faith continues to be possible only if those who suffer are given a different means of thinking about God.

CHAPTER FIVE

A Theology of Candor

Toward a Theology That Acknowledges Suffering Persists

"I must not turn this into poetry." That is the sentence which has been dinning itself into my mind as I have sat by the bedside of my dying father for the past several days. He has lain there, propped up against the pillows, his eyes closed, his strong frame shaking as his whole being has panted for breath. . . . Those groans are so deep that each of them sounds as though it must be the final one, all the breath available to him on this earth expended. They warn me that if anything is to be saved from this wreckage of a man it cannot come from outside this room; it cannot come from any subsequent poetry that glosses over the fearful fact that death is now bringing to an end the eighty years of my father's struggle for light against darkness.

—Donald Nicholl[1]

In attempting to find a different means of thinking about God, for many the Bible becomes the chief obstacle to a way forward. We tend to see what we expect to see when reading the Bible, and there are few points of view that cannot be supported by at least a verse here and there. So, with the images of God as both powerful and good in place, it is no surprise that some would argue that Scripture supports their point of view. And in popular parlance, to describe a point of view as biblical is to describe it as authoritative.

Some years ago as I began thinking about the subject of suffering, I gave a series of talks to a fairly large adult education class at a local church. The exchange was lively and it revealed just how deeply the triage theology that we each fashion takes hold of our hearts and minds. Many people were relieved to consider new ways of thinking about God and suffering. Older people in particular were grateful for an opportunity to talk about a subject that deeply troubled them, but which they did not feel free to explore. They feared that in raising questions they would upset those who were younger and looked up to them as "paragons of faith." So an "outsider" who gave them an opportunity to talk about the loss of friends and family, as well as their own frailty, was a welcome release. But not everyone felt that way.

Taking the Bible Seriously

Taking exception to much of what I had to say, one woman later wrote an impassioned letter:

> Your statement that "suffering is not God's will for us but occurs in the course of life," that God does not allow or permit suffering, implies that there are certain elements in life outside the control of God. This, as the class pointed out, calls into question God's total and complete sovereignty. In scripture I see a God who is uniquely in control, "exalting Himself as head above all" (1 Chronicles 29:11, 12). He is a God who does not pass the buck. He is ultimately responsible to bring things to right. If he is not in control of everything, including suffering, how will He perform all those things spoken of in Revelation?

Even though she agreed that any conversation about the subject of suffering should begin by acknowledging the pain and loss that people experience, it was clear from the outset that she felt there were certain facts about God and Scripture that must be accommodated. The balance of her rather lengthy letter was devoted to asserting that any conversation about the subject of suffering needs to preserve the sovereignty—the power, the complete control—of God. To her way of thinking, anything less was unbiblical and, therefore, unthinkable.

Since that time, I have become convinced that the primary obstacle to finding a new way of thinking about God and the problem of suffering often arises out of concerns similar to those raised in her letter. Many people hammer out their understanding of suffering constrained by what they believe the Bible teaches. They are neither ignorant nor unfeeling, but they do take their faith seriously and they believe that taking their faith seriously means taking the Bible seriously.

Beginning with the creation narrative, those same people often read the Bible as a story of divine power—its initial exercise, its expression in a perfect creation of something from nothing, its temporary frustration with the sin of humankind, and its final triumph thanks to God. If suffering occurs between creation and the end of all things it arises as a punishment for our sin, or as a tool of God's work in our lives. After all, so the reasoning goes, "God is great, God is good."

But this way of thinking about God and the problem of suffering is not the only possible way of reading the biblical text or of taking it seriously. Nor does the Bible explicitly defend this view. In fact, if we were going to argue that the Bible says anything of an explicit nature at all about this view of suffering, we would be forced to conclude that the Bible disapproves of it. The only place it receives a sweeping defense is on the lips of Job's comforters (e.g., Job 8:5–10), and their views are hardly cast in a positive light. Instead, the author tells a story of a righteous man who suffers deeply, setting the speeches of his comforters about sin and suffering against the backdrop of a situation that contradicts their view from the start (Job 1:1–2:13). "There was once a man in the land of Uz whose name was Job. That man was blameless and upright, one who feared God and turned away from evil."

Of course, what none of us find easy to admit is that the Bible doesn't actually offer an explicit, complete solution of any kind to the problem of suffering. The Bible is a collection of occasional literature, written by a variety of people, under widely varied sets of circumstances; and the books it contains were written over a very, very long period of time. It includes genealogies, stories, poetry, legal codes, letters, sermons, and fragments of liturgy. It is not a systematic statement of what we should believe.

Nor does the Bible clearly suggest how our beliefs should be woven into larger ways of thinking that we can apply to our lives. Like the lightning that illuminates the sky for a split second in one place, the Bible contains scattered intimations of God's nature and ways of being in the world that were brought to bear on specific concerns of a bygone era and preserved by the community of faith. But it does not provide a complete map of the night sky. That important, forever fragmentary, and imperfect task is left to us.

There is room, then, to imagine a very different picture of God and the problem of suffering that draws on other intimations from the biblical text. We need not begin with either the power or the goodness of God, and the history of the conversation about suffering suggests that it might be worth trying other possibilities.

So in what follows, I offer a different reading of the challenge posed by suffering. I will draw on Scripture and I take its contribution seriously. But I freely admit that the picture sketched below draws openly on other sources as well, including tradition, the contributions of others, my own reasoning, and importantly, an eye to as much of the human experience as possible.

For the sake of clarity, I have not attempted to identify the strands of reflection and reading that have contributed to every dimension of the views I have outlined here. Nor will I attempt to provide a lengthy defense of the views advanced here as compared with the considerable number of books that already exist on the subject. As a contribution to the triage theology

i.

At the heart of God is a passion for relationship.

ii.

Because of that passion, God imposes order on chaos,
and graces the created order with genuine autonomy.

iii.

God's creative work never ceases; yet chaos,
autonomy, and suffering all persist as well.

iv.

In granting autonomy, God surrenders a certain
degree of sovereignty, but continues to express
goodness in a relentless resolve to nurture
relationships.

v.

In the incarnation, through Jesus Christ, God
identifies with human suffering, affirms the
surrender (kenosis) of divine power, and
comprehends and transcends our experience
of suffering through death and resurrection.

that all of us shape, my goals are far more modest and essentially pastoral in nature. Based on our discussion thus far, you might think of the thoughts presented below as a series of God images that make candor and faith in God possible.

You will be the best judge of their value. This much I might say: the value of this or any other view depends in large part on its ability to remain candid about the suffering that we all experience. Here, then, in outline form are the elements in a theology of candor. Each point follows at length below. Because of the length and complexity of the observations made, at the end of each section I attempt to say something about the significance of the observations I have made for the problem of suffering and to raise questions that are explored later in the outline. That approach, in combination with the outline, will hopefully render the whole picture more accessible and helpful.

i. At the heart of God is a passion for relationship.

The passion for relationship is more basic to the nature of God than either power or goodness. It is at the heart of God's creative enterprise. It defines God's activity in the world. It is the desire that brings God both joy and despair. And it is this passion for relationship that shapes the way God is described elsewhere in both the Bible and our experience.

The opening chapters of Genesis alert us to this emphasis. Widely thought of as either a literal description of the creative process or as an ancient, mythic speculation on the origins of the universe, there are few books that are misread more often. But written in the period of the Exile, Genesis was not composed for either one of these reasons.[2]

Addressed to the sixth-century Jewish exiles living in Babylon, the writer—drawing on older traditions and stories—sought to reassure his readers that their faith in God was not misplaced, and offered reasons he hoped would bolster their determination to live faithfully. Deprived of their homeland and held captive by people of very different religious convictions, they experienced their own kind of persistent suffering and they had good reason to doubt the efficacy of their faith.

Over against the troubling realities of life in exile, the author affirms that God can be trusted, in spite of evidence to the contrary.[3] To that end, he describes a world created by God in the name of relationships—transcendent relationships embedded in the created order and enduring relationships with the people of God.

God's relational character is underlined in part through the way in which the creative act itself is described. The natural order is not denigrated, but it is clearly created for the benefit of humankind (Genesis 1:29–30). Adam and Eve are created last; they are given dominion over the rest of the animal kingdom (1:26); and they alone are created in God's image (1:26). The progression has the effect of focusing on the relationship between God and God's people.

But the author does not stop there. The nature of God's work extends to the relationship between humankind and the natural order, in that dominion implies responsibility (2:15). And the relational character of God's work is further underlined in the companionship and mutuality fostered in the creation of Eve (2:18).

As the author calls attention to the larger work of God that is the counterpoint to his readers' experience of exile, time and again he describes God's engagement in human affairs. God is walking in the garden and calls out for Adam and Eve when he discovers their disobedience (3:8); the blood of Cain calls out to God from the ground (4:10); and in seeking to salvage the relationships he has forged with humankind, God calls on Noah (6:13ff.), establishes a covenant with Abram (15:1ff.), renews the covenant with Jacob (28:10ff.), and moves in the dream life of Joseph (37:5ff.).

The author even dares to describe God as experiencing a range of emotional responses and a change of heart in the midst of this creative enterprise that can only be described as a capacity for pathos. God declares the created order "good" (1:31); walks in the garden "at the time of the evening breeze"

(3:8); and experiences sorrow in the face of human conduct during the days of Noah (6:6). In every case, the catalyst for God's pathos is relational and the response is the response of one who is passionate about the relationships won and lost with the people of God.

This emphasis on God's relational nature appears time and again in Scripture. But far from appearing in an isolated text here and there, the emphasis is, instead, basic to the content of both the Hebrew and Greek Testaments. The Pentateuch, or first five books of the Hebrew Testament, chronicle the work of a covenant-making God who formalizes a relationship with the nation of Israel and who, in giving the Law, seeks to create a religious and social space in which that relationship might flourish (Exodus 20:1ff.).

Repeatedly, the prophets remind the nation of the nature of that covenant and without hesitation underline the possible impact of the political decisions that are made on the shape of that relationship (Isaiah 30:1ff.). Even the concept of justice, which in popular contemporary speech has ethical and legal overtones, is for the God of Israel a relational concern, touching both Israel's relationship with its God and the relationship of Israelite with Israelite (Hosea 4:1ff.; see also Proverbs 14:31). To harm the poor is to jeopardize one's relationship with God (Jeremiah 22:15–16). And, as in the Book of Genesis, the prophets are familiar with God's passion for relationship (Jeremiah 31:2–3; Hosea 3:1ff.).

Since Jesus was a Jew, it is not surprising to find that he shares the same relational understanding of God, albeit expressed in slightly different language. The contexts for both his teaching and his conversations with his contemporaries are the same. God chose and created a covenant with Israel, and in three decisive moments nurtured that relationship: the call of Abram, the exodus from Egypt, and the gift of the Law.[4]

In the context of that conversation, Jesus underlines the relational character of God in three ways. In rich images often communicated in the form of parables, he first underlines the caring nature of God. The father of the prodigal son (Luke 15:11–32) and the shepherd of the sheep (Matthew 18:11–14; Luke 15:1–7) not only portray God as tirelessly relational, but also underline the extent to which God is prepared to preserve those relationships.

The same images and still others underscore a second emphasis in the teaching of Jesus on the individual. By no means does this feature of Jesus' teaching imply that he was uninterested in the covenantal and communal relationship in which God embraced the nation. But it is clear that alongside of that shared understanding, Jesus also understood God to be one who responded to the individual.

This emphasis on the relational is also pointed out in the teaching of Jesus as it applies to the kingdom of God. For the contemporaries of Jesus, one of the critical questions that faced the Jewish community revolved around the question of how to live as the people of God. For some, the vision of the future embraced a kingdom brought into being through force, one that emphasized the victor and the vanquished, the exclusivity of God's relationship with the nation. A second vision embraced a similar level of exclusivity, but maintained that exclusive character through a series of food laws and other observances that identified the boundaries in other ways. For Jesus, however, the kingdom is a contagion of mercy. His association with sinners and outcasts and his contact with Gentiles suggest a very different kind of kingdom, one in which the relational nature of God reaches out beyond the boundaries of those established by ethnic, political, and religious differences.[5]

It is little wonder, then, that the vast majority of names and descriptions attributed to God in both the Hebrew and Greek Testaments are relational and not abstract in character. Far from static virtues of some distant deity, the descriptions of God are focused instead on the relational nature of the encounter between God and humankind.

In the Hebrew Testament some of those names are rooted in specific relationships. Repeatedly, for example, the writers use the phrase "the God of Abraham, the God of Isaac, and the God of Jacob" (Exodus 3:5–7). Some names embrace the whole of the nation and so the phrase "the God of the Hebrews" (Exodus 10:2–4) is often used. Other descriptions highlight the capacity of God for the creation and nurture of those relationships. Repeatedly God is described as possessing *hesed* or steadfast faithfulness (Jeremiah 33:11; Psalm 100:5, 106:1; Ezra 3:11). Elsewhere God is described as one who fashions a covenant that will endure for generations, "an everlasting covenant" (Genesis 17:6–8), while still other adjectives focus on God's tireless quest to nurture and sustain those relationships in specific ways. So God is described as forgiving, merciful, and gracious (2 Chronicles 30:8–9; Nehemiah 9:30–32; Psalm 99:8–9).

Because the life of the church is rooted in the experience of the people of Israel, it is not surprising to find the same emphasis in the teaching of Jesus and his followers. They share in common some of the language for God. Many of the adjectives used to describe God find their counterpart in the Greek Testament (Acts 5:30–32; Romans 5:14–16; Ephesians 2:3–5) and many of the descriptions given of God revolve around God's capacity to forgive and to show mercy. We also can be sure that the images used by Jesus reflect a strong orientation to the nation of Israel, but like other Jews of his day, there are elements that stress the individual dimensions of a relationship with God. We already have noted some of the images that reinforce that picture. The father of the prodigal and the shepherd of the lost sheep invite relational understandings of God's activity that have an individual focus. But so, too, does the name Abba, which Jesus is described as having used as a means of referring to God as father (Mark 14:36).[6]

As the church slowly acquired its own religious consciousness, the language focused less in a matter-of-fact way on the life of the nation of Israel and more on the individual relationships that God forges with each person. But that language did not quickly or even completely disappear, and the language about God found in the Greek Testament remained relational in character. In one of the few absolute and seemingly abstract descriptions of God to found, even there the relational is key: "God is love" (1 John 4:7–9).

Significance for suffering

For those who suffer and believe in God, one of the most difficult challenges we can face arises out of questions about the role of God. If God is good, why doesn't God come to my aid? And if God is powerful, why doesn't God exercise that considerable power on my behalf? Is God just not there? Or did I do something to displease God? The difficulty in answering questions of this kind can plunge us into depression, precipitate a "crisis of faith," lead us to deny the reality of our suffering, or burden us with anxiety and guilt. But what if God isn't, first and foremost, about power—or even about goodness as we understand it? What if God's passion is the establishment of relationships?

At a minimum, goodness and power would be secondary characteristics of God and the priority we give to them would need to be reassessed. In addition, logically speaking it would not make sense to address the problem of suffering by grappling with the goodness and power of God as if they were all that mattered. It is here, then, with a God of relationships, that we must begin fashioning new God images, and with them in place, a different kind of triage theology.

ii. Because of that passion, God imposes order on chaos, and graces the created order with genuine autonomy.

God creates, then, with a view to establishing a web of relationships with the created order. The writer of Genesis is at pains to remind his readers of this. In exile the forces of chaos threaten the Israelite's sense of security. They have lost their homeland and with it, their identity. They are surrounded by conquerors who worship a different god and live in a way that is very different from their own. So the author of Genesis makes two points in telling his story. On the one hand, he underlines the temporary and deceptive nature of their losses; and, on the other hand, he stresses their responsibility to choose to be faithful.

In making the first point, the writer does not describe the engineered order of natural theology or arguments from design in which God creates a perfect something from nothing. Nor is that "perfect something of creation" lost through our sinfulness or a "fall" from grace. The tension between order and chaos is there from the beginning, and God's creative achievement is the assertion of order in the midst of chaos.

This is why the Book of Genesis does not begin with the words "In the beginning . . . was nothing," but begins instead with the words "In the beginning . . . the earth was a formless void and darkness covered the face of the deep." The author's readers know what chaos is and the "formless void" of creation is a candid means of describing the world in which they live.

The same phrase also captures in candid terms the way the people of the ancient Near East experienced the world around them. Living where fertile land was limited and the well-being of whole civilizations was affected by changes in the weather, it was the ability of a god to assert order and control over the ever-present chaos that constituted the great creative act. The existence of "something" was taken for granted.[7] The existence of order was not.

So the writer of Genesis reminds the exiled children of Israel that in the beginning God brought order. God gave the "formless void" that covered the earth its boundaries. Dry earth appeared. Day and night were distinguished. Order was established. Chaos may have its day, but God can be counted on to establish its boundaries and order the world yet again.

This realization hardly absolves the author's readers of responsibility. It actually magnifies those responsibilities. God's passion for relationship cannot be satisfied by coercion or by engineering a world without chaos in which we can live. The creation in all its dimensions requires autonomy, if relationships are to exist or thrive.

We need to read the story of Eden, then, without the lenses of a centuries-long discussion of "the fall." Adam and Eve are not the primeval couple making a decision on behalf of human history and experience. They are not the architects of our destiny. They represent the human condition and they possess the power to choose a relationship with God or reject it, just as we do. Our lives shape the story of Adam and Eve, not the other way around.

Nor does this freedom extend to human beings alone. The passion that God is said to have for relationships with Adam and Eve extends to the natural order as well. The writer describes God's creative work as both "direct and indirect," as a process in which God both "makes things" and lures the creation to "make things." God's passion for relationship is so great, and autonomy is so essential to the nurture of those relationships, that God risks sharing the creative power to bring order in the midst of chaos with the creation itself.[8]

Significance for suffering

When we suffer, we often struggle as much with the "fact" of our suffering as we do with the particulars of it. Someone married for a quarter of a century struggles with the shards of a broken life after a divorce—legal proceedings, mounting bills, caring for children, attempting to recover some sense of self-worth. She didn't want a divorce, didn't expect a divorce, didn't deserve a divorce. Someone else struggles with the onslaught of a fatal disease. Yesterday (and even today) he feels fine. He was making responsible plans for the future, living, loving, and working. Now the sun has suddenly set. The days and hours of life that are left can almost be counted.

In the midst of these experiences and others, at some level we simply find it difficult to believe that suffering can intrude in this way on our lives and the lives of those we love. Part of that response is simply shock, of course. We necessarily labor to absorb the news that we sometimes receive. But on another level, I've often sensed that we struggle with what we might call "utopian" views of life. When suffering persists, we don't simply find it difficult to "take it all in": we didn't expect it to happen at all.

Part of this utopian view is uniquely American. We are compulsively visionary about our lives, collectively and individually. We expect to transcend challenges and to create a better world. But another engine of our utopian outlook can be traced to the triage theologies that we fashion. If we live in what was once a complete and perfect world, then the "fact" of suffering is all the more difficult to accommodate, emotionally, spiritually, and intellectually. Something or someone is to blame.

But the Book of Genesis and the picture of creation we find there suggest that chaos was a given at the very beginning; and so, too, was the potential dislocation traceable to the autonomy we are given to exercise. And, if you think about it, the picture given to us was passed along by someone writing to exiled Israelites who already knew that was the case. Such an insight may not spare us the pain, grief, and mourning that accompanies suffering, and it may not help us to take it in. But it may spare us the added struggle to find someone or something to blame for suffering that we are convinced should not have happened at all.

iii. God's creative work never ceases; yet chaos, autonomy, and suffering all persist as well.

Creation and the ordering of chaos is not just a moment in the past, however. For ancient Judaism the creative process continues. The story begun by the writer of Genesis culminates with the creation of Adam and Eve. But it ends there in order to bring the readers of Genesis to the point where they can clearly see their situation mirrored in the lives of this "primeval" couple. It does not mean that the creative task of ordering the world is at an end.

The waters of chaos are confined to boundaries set by God, but they have not disappeared. Ever-present in the days of Noah, they threaten to overwhelm the created order once again:

> In the six hundredth year of Noah's life, in the second month, on the seventeenth day of the month, on that day all the fountains of the great deep burst forth, and the windows of the heavens were opened. (Genesis 7:11)[9]

Noah, like Adam, epitomizes the challenge that Israel's exiled faithful face. His day is like their day. There is God. There is chaos. There is the challenge to obedience. By contrast, however, Noah models the righteousness that Adam does not. In pairing the two story cycles, the writer underlines how little difference there is between the first seven days and any that follow. Chaos persists. So too does suffering.

The chaos that is beaten back by God in the Book of Genesis appears again in the psalms:

> You made the deep cover the earth as a garment.
> The waters stood above the mountains.
> They fled at Your blast,
> Rushed away at the sound of Your thunder,
>   —mountains rising, valleys sinking—
>   to the place You established for them.
> You set bounds they must not pass so that they
>   never again cover the earth.
>   (Psalm 104:6–9)[10]

The same theme appears in the Book of Job and the prophets.

> Awake, awake, put on strength, O arm of the LORD!
> Awake, as in the days of old, the generations of long ago!
> Was it not you who cut Rahab in pieces, who pierced the dragon?

> Was it not you who dried up the sea, the waters of the
> great deep;
> who made the depths of the sea a way for the redeemed to
> cross over?
> So the ransomed of the LORD shall return,
> and come to Zion with singing; everlasting joy shall be
> upon their heads;
> they shall obtain joy and gladness, and sorrow and
> sighing shall flee away.
> (Isaiah 51:9–11)

Israel is convinced of God's steadfast faithfulness and of God's final victory, but chaos continues to violate the boundaries that God has set for it and, as a result, suffering persists. Suffering cannot necessarily be traced to sin (although ancient Israel knew sin and its identifiable consequences). Its cause lies elsewhere.

The same theme appears in the Greek Testament. In Romans 8, for example, Paul paints a picture of cosmic dislocation and long-awaited redemption. He writes:

> I consider that the sufferings of this present time are not
> worth comparing with the glory about to be revealed to
> us. For the creation waits with eager longing for the
> revealing of the children of God; for the creation was
> subjected to futility, not of its own will but by the will of
> the one who subjected it, in hope that the creation itself
> will be set free from its bondage to decay and will obtain
> the freedom of the glory of the children of God. We
> know that the whole creation has been groaning in labor
> pains until now; and not only the creation, but we our-
> selves, who have the first fruits of the Spirit, groan
> inwardly while we wait for adoption, the redemption of
> our bodies. For in hope we were saved. Now hope that is
> seen is not hope. For who hopes for what is seen? But if
> we hope for what we do not see, we wait for it with
> patience. (Romans 8:18–25)

Significance for suffering

The biblical text is prescientific in every respect. It is an interpretive mistake to treat the contents of Genesis, Romans, or any other part of the Bible as if it had been written with the apparatus of twenty-first-century science in mind. So, to see evolutionary science in the picture described there, or to read it looking for evidence to the contrary, is a profound mistake.

But the picture in Genesis of an ongoing creative process and Paul's notions of cosmic redemption provide theological language that invite a conversation with evolutionary science. At first blush, this may not seem important for a discussion of suffering. But to the extent that the unevenness of the evolutionary process, natural disasters, and other events contribute to the suffering in our world, the invitation to a conversation between theological and scientific categories is of sweeping significance.

As science has deepened our understanding of the world around us, we have become aware of the extent to which much of what shapes our lives is woven in unseen ways into our world. Forces as different as the genetic origins of disease and the climactic changes that have influenced life on entire continents are just two examples of the ways in which the suffering we experience can be traced to dynamics that are woven into the fabric of the world around us and within us. Sickle-cell anemia, Parkinson's disease, and a wide variety of cancers shape the lives of young and old. Forces of this kind cannot be traced to the choices we make, nor can they be explained with artful references to divine providence.

Nonetheless, as people of faith we often resist this conclusion. We fear that to grant that suffering of this kind might be rooted in forces as impersonal and seemingly unpredictable as our genetic makeup could also banish God from our world. As a result, we continue to struggle with other explanations, or we live uneasily in two worlds, embracing a mix of scientific and religious views without any clear notion of how they might fit together.

The invitation to a dialogue between the language of evolutionary science and a faith that embraces the ongoing, creative work of God can help to address those concerns. It can also create an opening for greater candor about our experience of the world, allow us to speak in theological terms that honor the world as it is, spare us the search for explanations for suffering that are rooted in misplaced guilt and eliminate the need to theologize the causes of illness and disaster.

iv. In granting autonomy, God surrenders a certain degree of sovereignty, but continues to express goodness in a relentless resolve to nurture relationships.

By committing to the creation of a world capable of a relationship with its creator, God also commits to certain profound constraints. Because of this commitment, the power God possesses to order chaos is evident in broken and fragmentary ways that cannot be expressed in a more obvious fashion. It is love yearning for relationship, expressed in both command and the capacity for mercy that God expresses in the fabric of the world around us and in the experiences of the people of God.

As such God is both immanent (or nearby and one with the reality around us) and transcendent (lying beyond our ordinary experience of reality). God possesses the power to shape the created order in a fashion that needs relationship, but is unable to coerce us or nature into that relationship. Acting persuasively instead, God is present with us in the brokenness of a world that only partially recognizes its need of God.

The greatness of God is not manifested, then, in an all-dominating, controlling fashion, or in an obvious display of power. Instead, the greatness of God is manifested in the ability and willingness to respond endlessly to our choices—good, bad, and indifferent. The direction that God can and does provide in our midst is less obvious than the divine sovereignty of other theologies.

To offer a metaphor that goes at least some way toward explaining the difference, the contrast might be explained using an ocean-going illustration (making allowances for the fact that I am not now, nor ever have been, a sailor!). With that caveat: on a more obvious reading of divine activity in the world, God is like a large ship propelled through the water by an engine. The engine, and with it, the rudder of the ship, is determinative for direction and speed. An engine-propelled ship is less dependent upon currents and weather; the course it can steer is more nearly a straight line between two points.

A God of relationships is at work in the world in a way that is more immediately analogous to the behavior of a sailboat. Dependent on a number of variables, including currents and the wind, God responds to the contingencies of our lives, tacking first this way and then that. The ship may travel between the same two spots on the map as that traveled by an engine-driven vessel, but the course is not at all straight. It is marked by serendipity and, from time to time, tragedy.

God is, by virtue of this difference, not less great, but differently greater. God's goodness is also redefined, but not in abstract terms. Instead, the goodness of God is defined in terms of God's passion for relationship and willingness to endure the ragged edges of a world in which the ongoing nature of creation, the continued presence of chaos, and the variables introduced by autonomy shape the world in which God seeks us.

Significance for suffering
On this reading of the biblical message, a very different God image emerges at the forefront of our theology. If God is no longer "out there" wielding power, then it is no longer necessary to explain why a good God would allow the human experience to unfold in the way that it does. Indeed, there is a sense in which the ragged edges of human life and the suffering that occurs are descriptive of a process that simply is what it is: the world God intends, coming into being. This approach to the

problem is also particularly helpful, because it allows us to acknowledge the reality of the pain and loss of those who suffer.

As candor begins to set in, it becomes clear that an exclusive emphasis on the power of God is, in fact, nonsensical in the face of what the Bible is at greatest pains to say about the nature of God. Although God is described in both testaments as loving, merciful, steadfast, faithful, and forgiving, it becomes clear that the revealed theology of both the Jewish and Christian traditions places far greater emphasis on other characteristics of God.

In the Hebrew Testament, for example, the "steadfast faithfulness" or *hesed* of God is the basis of the covenantal relationship with the children of Israel. Undeterred by their choices, the prophetic and poetical record reminds the people time and again of God's enduring love. The prophet Hosea is even prepared to describe God as the ever-caring husband of a prostitute. In spite of her choices, God continues to love Israel, acknowledging in the name the prophet gives to their child both the choices the nation makes and God's *hesed*.

> When she had weaned Lo-ruhamah, she conceived and bore a son. Then the LORD said, "Name him Lo-ammi, for you are not my people and I am not your God."
>
> Yet the number of the people of Israel shall be like the sand of the sea, which can be neither measured nor numbered; and in the place where it was said to them, "You are not my people," it shall be said to them, "Children of the living God."[11]

In the Greek Testament the same notion is echoed over and over. But few are as absolute in their equation of God with love as the writer of the First Epistle of John, who flatly asserts, "God is love."[12]

Given this emphasis, even if it were possible to argue that God is all-powerful, it remains a largely abstract and meaningless assertion. It is clear that God's ability to act would, at a minimum, be circumscribed by the demands of love, mercy, faithfulness, and forgiveness and, if that is the case, then God cannot do anything.

The picture becomes even more complex if you allow for authentic human choices. If the order God asserts over the chaos that is life necessitates human choice, and if that choice, pitted against God, can even have a dislocating impact on that order, then an obvious sovereignty cannot be defended. It also becomes impossible to hold that everything that happens is God's doing or happens by virtue of God's permission. Only a thoroughgoing determinism or choices that only appear to be choices could fit with such notions of divine control.

v. In the incarnation, through Jesus Christ, God identifies with human suffering, affirms the surrender (kenosis) of divine power, and comprehends and transcends our experience of suffering through death and resurrection.

The suffering and death of Jesus emerges at the center of this very different constellation of God images.[13] Jesus identifies with humanity in its peril and frailty;[14] embraces the surrender or *kenosis* of divine power in the incarnation;[15] and is, by virtue of that surrender, able to comprehend and transcend our experience.[16]

We are so accustomed to reading the ancient creeds that begin with the creative activity of God that we find it difficult to hear this point at all. For that reason, it is something of a theological misfortune that the two best-known creeds, the Apostles' Creed and the Nicene Creed, begin in that fashion.[17] When Christians have struggled with the divine and human natures of Christ, contrary to popular belief, they have struggled far more often with the latter than the former. This is why, for example, books like Nikos Kanzantzakis's *The Last Temptation of Christ* (and the film by Martin Scorcese) have proven so controversial.[18] Bracketed by notions of divinity (in the case of temptation) and power (in the case of suffering), the redemptive work of Christ has an "as if" quality for many people. "Jesus was tempted, but couldn't surrender to temptation."

"Jesus suffered and died, but he was about to be resurrected." Completely missing is any sense of real jeopardy or sacrifice.

But to read the incarnation in these terms fails to grasp that the peril in temptation is the ability to surrender and the peril in suffering lies in genuine loss, meaninglessness, and the pain that accompanies it. The problem with our readings of the divine drama may have little or nothing to do with the notion of transcendence, but has to do instead with our failure to read the story as it is told to us. If we do read it as it is told to us, then we are invited into a redemptive drama marked by the genuine surrender of power and the fullest experience of human suffering.

What is needed, then, is a confession of faith that so strongly identifies the suffering of Jesus with the suffering of humanity that the sense of peril, loss, pain, and meaninglessness is as complete as ours. Once we are candid, this is both what we can see and what we need to hear in the story of Jesus. To some degree it may be easier to hear it anew in a story that intersects in instructive ways with the gospel:

> George Harley was a missionary who, along with his pregnant wife, was sent to Monrovia, Liberia. Having studied tropical medicine at Duke University and the University of London, he moved into that country's interior in order to provide medical care for the native tribes living there. Years later, he was asked by a bishop to describe the first four or five years of his work and ministry there.
>
> Harley explained, "Bishop, we built a dispensary and a chapel and then I began to treat the people's illnesses. But I soon realized that, although they were ready to receive what medical assistance I was willing to give them, the people were not prepared to hear the gospel. So, for months and then for years, my wife, my son and I worshipped alone at the chapel.
>
> "Then one day, as I watched him in a nearby field, I saw my son run, fall; run again, fall; and run a third time,

only to fall again. I went out to help him and discovered that he was burning up with a fever. In the following days, I brought everything I had learned to bear upon finding a cure to his disease but, in a matter of days, he died.

"I built a small, rudely made coffin for my son and began to walk through the village to a cemetery on the other side. On my way, the village blacksmith said, 'Is that your son?' And when I acknowledged that it was, he said, 'I reckon he's heavy, I'll give you a hand.' So the blacksmith and I carried my son to the cemetery.

"But there, when we finished the grave, I was so overcome with grief and with a sense of isolation that I buried my face in the freshly dug earth and began to cry. Only slowly did I become aware that the blacksmith had begun to run back toward the village, screaming at the top of his voice, 'The white man cries like we cry! The white man cries like we cry!'

"On the following Sunday, for the first time in four years, my family did not worship alone. The chapel and grounds around it were crowded with the people from the village."

The bishop looked at Harley and said, "Do you mean, George, that it was only with the loss of your son that the people finally responded to your message?" And Harley replied, "Yes, and I suddenly realized that it was this sacrifice that God made for us."[19]

The story is one with colonial overtones, of course, dating as it does to another time. Thankfully we have taught one another that we can cry and that, by inference, God cries with all of us. But the window into both the peril and the sacrifice embraced by Jesus at the heart of Harley's story can bring hope to people who experience the world as it is.

In turn, Jesus' radical identification with us requires that we also think of resurrection as God's "no" to death, but a "no" that takes place only after the full effect of death has taken its toll. It is not the moment to which the life and ministry of Jesus leads. To think of it in those terms is to reintroduce the "as if" character of the way we read his life.

Death is not a mere vehicle to eternal life, a portal, a door, or a part of the "intended" order of things. It is dark and meaningless. Writing to his father at the time of his mother's death, Henri Nouwen observes:

> As I reflect on mother's death, something that I could not see as clearly as before is now becoming more visible to me. It is that death does not belong to God. God did not create death. God does not want death. God does not desire death for us. In God there is no death. God is a God of life. He is the God of the living and not of the dead. Therefore, people who live a deeply spiritual life, a life of real intimacy with God, must feel the pain of death in a particularly acute way. A life with God opens us to all that is alive. It makes us celebrate life; it enables us to see the beauty of all that is created; it makes us desire to always be where life is. Death, therefore, must be experienced by a really religious person neither as a release from the tension of life nor as an occasion for rest and peace, but as an absurd, ungodly, dark nothingness. Now I see why it is false to say that a religious person would find death easy and acceptable. Now I understand why it is wrong to think that a death without struggle and agony is a sign of great faith. These ideas do not make much sense once we realize that faith opens us to the full affirmation of life and gives us an intense desire to live more fully, more vibrantly, and more vigorously. *If anyone should protest against death it is the religious person, the person who has increasingly come to know God as the God of the living.*[20]

Having said this, because Christ enters deeply and completely into the experience of death, the resurrection is also a decisive answer to our experience. To borrow the words of theologian Donald Nicholl as he reflected on the approaching death of his father, what God accomplishes in the incarnation is not poetry. Nor is anything that is saved from the wreckage of our lives saved from outside the room. God breaks the hold that chaos has on our lives from within, responds to the chaos unleashed by the autonomy we are given, and thereby offers us a new alternative through the resurrection.[21]

Affirmations of the Candid

This, then, sets the stage for us to acknowledge certain realities about the nature of suffering that only the candid can acknowledge.[22]

God does not will suffering. It occurs in the course of life.
If God enters deeply into our existence, then the testimony of those who believe is that believing does not insure immunity from suffering. The faithful face adversity, illness, and death; and the suffering that accompanies them is at odds with the nature and will of God. God enters deeply into that suffering, conquering it only after experiencing it, through the power of the resurrection. God's compassion is expressed in the only way possible, by entering into that suffering with us, not in ultimately delivering us from it.

It is a mistake, therefore, to look for a hidden purpose or reason in the suffering we experience. We may bring some suffering on ourselves through our own sinfulness; and we may inflict suffering on others through the same sinfulness. But not all suffering will yield to an explanation of this kind.

As such, the spiritual well-being of the candid faithful is grounded in the confidence that God is present to us—even in the midst of experiences marked by cruelty or loss. Aware of the choices modeled from within the room, we sink into the arms of the one who is "God with us," confident in the knowledge that God knows our world on intimate terms.

God does not use suffering in order to teach us, although we may learn through it. Nor does God use suffering to strengthen us, although this too may happen.

Suffering "radically simplifies" life, and in those moments, the distractions and superficiality of our lives often undergo considerable scrutiny.[23] Out of that dynamic, some people grow and deepen spiritually and emotionally. Sadly, others are overwhelmed. I count among my dear and good friends those who have had both experiences.

The results cannot be charted in any easy fashion, tracing spiritual and moral strength or courage. The variables include the autobiographical character of their struggle, their life histories, the nature and intensity of the suffering they experience, and the lessons they are able (or unable) to draw from the experience. Some who suffer are well supported and loved, others are not. Still others are surrounded by love, but because of depression are unaware of it.

There are, then, significant variables, and where good arises, in spite of the circumstances, the power of the resurrection is at work. But the experiences themselves are at odds with the loving intention of God, and as consoling as it might be to argue that a hidden purpose is at work in the experience of suffering itself, it is a mistake to suggest this is the case. To deny that the suffering is real, and in and of itself tragic, is to minimize the pain of others. It also pits the tragic circumstances faced by one person against the circumstances faced by another.

God does not depend on human suffering to achieve God's purposes but through it God's purposes are sometimes achieved.

Much of the misunderstanding here arises from proof-texting that well known passage from Romans 8:28: "We know that all things work together for good for those who love God, who are called according to his purpose." As I've already said, based on this passage many Christians argue that God "orchestrates" our suffering. If he does not actively will it, they argue, then God at least permits it. This, however, is to misread the passage in more than one way.

First, the reading is completely at odds with Paul's purpose in Romans 8. Paul has just finished painting a picture of the all-embracing redemption that awaits both the church and the world. He paints that picture as one characterized by "labor pains" and "eager longing." In other words, the church awaits the realization of God's "good" will—the torturous experience is *not* God's will. It is the chaos from which the believer can hope to be delivered.

This is also borne out by the language of the passage itself: Romans 8:28 reads, "all things work together for good"—*not* all things are good. It may seem to be a small difference, but it is a critical difference, nonetheless.[24]

Paul's picture, then, is not of miseries tailor-made by God for realizing divine purposes. The events are at odds with God's will. The power of God is manifested, instead, in the transformation of those events.

The biblical pattern is not the one, then, that our society emphasizes. It is not a pattern of easy deliverance, nor is it a pattern that redefines our suffering as something other than what it is. Indeed, transformation is at the heart of the gospel. The death and resurrection of Jesus is a triumph over sin and death. It is triumph "in spite of suffering," not "through" it.[25]

That resurrection power is, in its definitive form, God's alone. But as part of the resurrected community, it is already ours. The childless adopt the orphan; the broken manifest God's mercy; those who grieve teach others to trust; those who are persecuted preach the full measure of justice. The lessons learned, the compassion expressed, and the justice achieved are realized not because the losses were not real, but because those who experienced them remained alive to the presence of God.[26]

CHAPTER SIX

Embracing the Suffering of Others

Creating a Caring Community

I can't tell you what it feels like, to have your own sickness be the source of a false alarm. Everyone is making a big fuss and watching, and you bear the responsibility for wasting the time of professionals who might truly be needed elsewhere—and then there are the quick micro-glances of skepticism, the up-and-down evaluation: Is he really drunk or high? Is he being punished for yesterday's pleasures? . . . Then, of course, there were the Christian reactions, no less complicated. Prayer is an obvious response to illness; and if the illness is a broken leg or fever, it should not feel condemning. But if the sickness is a part of your very formation, it can also feel like a rejection of who you are, who you have to be. To hurry up and pray for a Down's syndrome child may be an expression of your own revulsion; it may be an indication of your anxiety, not his need. And those of us who were broken right from the start, we don't know how to say any of this without being told that we're wrong, wrong, wrong, we just want your healing.
—Bill Williams[1]

In our professionalized world, formal preparation dominates. We atomize life, breaking it down into discrete tasks. Then we design the training needed to perform the tasks. Credentials follow. They are given to those who are trained and serve as a means of distinguishing those who can and cannot perform certain tasks. It is a practice that has allowed us to create a complex society in which we deal successfully with the demands of modern life.

But there is a danger inherent in this approach. The professionalization of life's tasks inevitably creates a climate in which we think of some very natural roles that we should all fulfill as the special roles of a few. Someone with training. Someone with credentials. Caregivers give care. Why should we?

Over the years I have been called on to fulfill one of those specialized roles. I have visited and prayed with people facing unemployment and fatal disease. I have comforted and advised young families in crisis and couples long married. I have been present at the funerals of the elderly and those who have died suddenly in tragic accidents. And in each of those cases, I am confident that training can be of enormous value.

But here is the truth: in the moment of crisis, there is a kind of caring that can only be given by those whose lives are already rooted in the lives of those who suffer. Shared ties, experience, "history," sorrows, and joys weave relationships that no professional can duplicate in a few hours or days. And like the power of our bodies to heal wounds, those relationships have the power to bring us healing and peace. To recognize this fact is to recognize that we rely on the relationships that God seeks to nurture with us and among us. So how do the candid faithful create a caring community?

They Resist Claiming to "Know" What Others Are Experiencing.

The commonalties of human life represent the rich fabric around which we build our lives. Shared experiences make the language of care and nurture possible, and help to reduce our sense of isolation. As trust and love grow, much of the communication between two people can take place even in silence; and depending on the circumstances, those commonalties can bind ever larger groups of people together. But suffering has an irreducibly autobiographical character shaped by the personal history that we bring to the experience of loss, bereavement, or tragedy. To comfort someone else requires careful attention to that autobiography, to the particular shape that it takes, and to the way in which grief, loss, and disappointment intersect in someone's life.

To claim that "we know" what someone else is experiencing claims too much. It planes the rough edges off our own experience and loses the specifics of someone else's needs. The commonalities that enrich our communication become the basic features of a shorthand diagnosis. As a result, we foreclose on the process of listening. We no longer hear the particulars, the specific way in which one experience of suffering is not quite like the last, and we stop listening, even if the person we seek to comfort continues talking.

Yet, it is in listening carefully and attentively that we affirm our love for those around us. The willingness to move into someone else's world, particularly at a time when they are experiencing grief, affirms that they are loved in a way that extends beyond our need for companionship and is rooted in unconditional care for the one who suffers.

They Resist Explaining away the Agony of Those Who Struggle with Loss.

As hard as it may be at times, try to remember that reactions shaped by your own discomfort are unlikely to be helpful to those who suffer. In order to confront a need, we must first be able to acknowledge and fully face its existence. To explain away the agony of someone else short-circuits that effort.

Psychologists who deal with grief and mourning identify two kinds of loss, primary and secondary. Primary losses are the immediate, presenting losses that we experience: divorce, death, the loss of a job, or a debilitating illness. However, in the wake of those experiences we often incur secondary losses as well. When we lose a spouse, for example, we often lose a "lover, best friend, helpmate, confidant, coparent, social partner, housemate, traveling companion, business associate, career supporter, auto repair person, housekeeper, and 'other half.'"[2] In addition, we lose certain dreams and ways of thinking, an inner dialogue that shapes much of the way in which we see the world around us.

It is only by having a safe space to recognize, name, and confront those losses that we can grieve and mourn properly. The ability to tell our stories and to name our losses in prayer is fundamental to weaving them into the fabric of our lives; and it is only in so doing that we can begin to "relearn the world"[3] that has changed around us. Conversely, to minimize those losses or to suggest that the losses are simply a means to an end effectively silences those who suffer and brings the process of relearning the world to a close.

A candid community values the process of listening and can absorb the complexity of loss without explaining away the agony of those who struggle with it. Their prayers embrace the one who suffers; the community creates a space in which the one who suffers can find healing in new relationships with God and with other persons; and, together, the community testifies to the enduring significance of those relationships. Those who experience persistent suffering thereby relearn the world and find hope, knowing that God still inhabits the world in which they live.

They Resist Easy Answers.

Years ago Shell Oil Company featured the "Shell Answer Man" as part of a national advertising campaign. Armed with easy answers to easy questions, he defined the word *viscosity*, extolled the virtues of regular engine maintenance, and advised listeners about the direct relationship between the weight of a vehicle and gas mileage. The campaign promoted a gentle if paternalistic image of the company, the care and attention it gave to its products, and confidence in the company's mastery of the details.

It is easy for all of us to believe that to care for someone who suffers requires that we provide confident answers to their questions and solutions for their problems. The can-do, problem-solving character of our culture predisposes us to the conviction that the best possible assistance that we can provide anyone is to fix the problem or find an answer. As we have already seen, however, it is not at all easy to find answers or solutions; and none of the workable answers are likely to be at all simple.

A caring community sets aside its need to project an image of competence and can content itself with the task of caring. Simple answers, if accepted at all, are likely to fail the people to whom we give them. If and when they do, those who rely on them are likely to experience grief added to grief.

They Resist Rushing the One Who Suffers to Closure.

The last quarter of a century has seen tremendous growth in study devoted to the issues of loss, grief, and mourning. What emerges strongly from the literature is the realization that the language of steps, stages, and tasks does not provide a helpful window into the experience of those who grieve or mourn. Some of that literature also makes an important distinction between "grief" (understood as the experience of loss) and "mourning" (as the psychosocial process needed to adapt in the face of a loss). In a sense, grief is something we experience quickly, but mourning can be a lengthy experience that might not ever be "completed" in any absolute sense of the word.[4]

It is far more accurate to talk about the identifiable experiences that are needed to relearn the world around us in the face of persistent suffering or loss. Those experiences include opportunities to:

- recognize the loss we have experienced;
- react to the separation that occurs;
- recollect and re-experience the person and the relationship;
- relinquish the old attachments to both the person and the relationship;
- readjust, moving adaptively into the new world without forgetting the old;
- reinvest.[5]

We may not do this in any prescribed order. Indeed, we probably won't; and the experiences will overlap and intersect. But they are necessary to our well-being, and anyone who grieves will need to have these experiences.

To rush people to closure overlooks their need to mourn and potentially pathologizes a natural and necessary process. It also overlooks the relational character of the loss. We can only emotionally and spiritually navigate a loss of that kind; it will not go away.

The danger in rushing someone to closure is even more evident when you take into account the complex landscape of grief and mourning itself. The same research that has helped us to see that there is nothing linear about our experience has also uncovered profound differences in the complexity of those losses. In attempting to describe the differences, clinical psychologists distinguish between two kinds of grief, uncomplicated and complicated mourning.[6] The labels are the ones used by clinicians and they are not meant to suggest that any grieving is "uncomplicated" as such. But the basic distinction that they make underlines the complexity of grief in general.

When we experience uncomplicated mourning, we are able to encounter the emotions that accompany our loss without being overwhelmed. As the list above suggests, we are able to "recognize the loss we have experienced; react to the separation that occurs; recollect and re-experience the person and the relationship that we have lost; relinquish the old attachments to both the person and the relationship; readjust, moving adaptively into the new world without forgetting the old; and, eventually, reinvest" in the world and people around us.

If we are unable to do any of the things described above, or if we are overwhelmed in the attempt to grapple with our loss, then we enter into an arena that researchers call complicated mourning. Broadly speaking, those who experience mourning of this kind are attempting to do one of two things. They either repress their grief and its implications, or they hold on to the one who is lost.[7]

There are two sets of factors that may lead a person to respond in this way. One set revolves around the circumstances of the death itself. Suicide, as well as unexpected, violent, or accidental death, can truncate the grieving of those who are left behind. Each raises special issues that demand attention, but distracts from the energy that the loss itself would normally require. Feelings of anger, betrayal, and abandonment can mark the aftermath of a suicide. Unexpected deaths can create challenges that absorb a family's energy and resources as they scramble to adjust financially. And those who struggle with the loss of a loved one to violent or accidental death can become burdened by a knowledge of the way in which a friend or family member died.

Death from a prolonged illness, the loss of a child, and the perception that a death might have been prevented can also raise issues that demand attention, but also complicate mourning. Cases of this kind, like those listed above, can be overshadowed by litigation for months or even years. The time and energy that might have been focused on mourning often is spent instead negotiating the frustrating waters of American jurisprudence.

A second set of factors is associated with circumstances that arise before or after the death. Relationships marked by anger, dependence, or ambivalence can raise issues that take center stage. Those who grieve may be suffering from mental health problems. Still others may find it difficult to find the time to mourn, because they are forced to cope with injuries or illness of their own. This is particularly true in the case of natural disasters, accidents, or an epidemic in which the lives of people close to one another are all affected at the same time.

An ever larger number of people also may feel unsupported by the communities around them. This feeling may arise in part from the ever larger and more mobile communities in which many of us live. Establishing friendships of any kind can prove to be difficult. Establishing deeper, nurturing relationships can be all but impossible, given the modern shape of life and work in urban areas.

In addition, more and more people are experiencing what clinicians refer to as "disenfranchised" grief.[8] Coping with losses that go unacknowledged by the people around them, they may have meaningful relationships, but the people they know may not recognize their grief as grief.

Miscarriage, for example, has long been the occasion for disenfranchised grief. People will quickly respond, "You can always try again." They fail to recognize that people prepare an emotional, if not physical, space in their lives for a child. For that reason, a child lost through miscarriage often has all the claim on the parents' affection that a newborn might have. People also overlook the possibility that a miscarriage is indicative of still other, long-term difficulties that may make "trying again" impossible.

Disenfranchised grief can take other forms, however, some of which can bring with it added alienation. AIDS victims, for example, often have been subjected to cruel and punishing treatment. Not only are they denied the support of a community, they often are told that their illness and even the death of those close to them are an instrument of divine judgment. Aggressively disenfranchised, they are left with a burden that goes well beyond the simple effort to identify a caring community.

To rush the one who suffers to closure often ignores the complex and far-from-mechanical nature of mourning, and potentially complicates the mourning that each of us needs to experience. Nor is death the only occasion for experiences of this kind. A caring community is alert to the needs of those around them that come with other "endings." The loss of a job, a loved one with Alzheimer's disease, cancer, divorce, and any number of other experiences can precipitate a similarly complex set of needs.

They Resist Weighing the Spiritual Maturity/Worth of Those Who Suffer Based upon Their Response.

Everything I have said up to this point should also lay to rest any assumption that those who struggle in times of suffering are spiritually deficient. No one is exempt from mourning a lost loved one, but there are other losses as well. The psalms of disorientation are an excellent example.

Hear my prayer, O LORD;
    let my cry come to you.
Do not hide your face from me
    in the day of my distress.
Incline your ear to me;
    answer me speedily in the day when I call.

For my days pass away like smoke,
    and my bones burn like a furnace.
My heart is stricken and withered like grass;
    I am too wasted to eat my bread.
Because of my loud groaning
    my bones cling to my skin.
I am like an owl of the wilderness,
    like a little owl of the waste places.
I lie awake;
    I am like a lonely bird on the housetop.
        (Psalm 102:1–7)

This psalm is illustrative of a pattern to be found elsewhere in Scripture—in Psalms, Job, Ecclesiastes, Jeremiah, Lamentations, and the Gospels. The biblical text is brutally frank about suffering. It does not engage in indirection. It does not indulge in euphemisms. It openly acknowledges pain, hurt, suffering, and disorientation; and it is not afraid to acknowledge them in equally frank language to both God and other people.

But the features that are missing from psalms of disorientation (and other parts of Scripture) are as instructive as the features that do appear. There is no self-sufficient stoicism, no easy believism, no quick dismissal of pain, no assertion that deliverance is guaranteed. Nor does the psalmist suggest that deliverance can be had by means of positive confession. What we have is simply ragged, painful confession—not unlike the picture given by the evangelists of Jesus' prayer in the garden of Gethsemane (Matthew 26:36–46; Mark 14:32–42; Luke 22:39–46). If painless, confident endurance of suffering is the measure of genuine faith, then the evangelists could have done far better than they did in portraying Jesus as he faced the prospect of crucifixion.

Where Suffering is the Result of Human Cruelty or Callousness, the Candid Faithful Acknowledge Our Role, Identify the Causes, and Oppose Them.

On the face of it this affirmation would seem to be obvious enough. In fact, however, we often minimize the suffering that human cruelty causes by arguing that somehow larger goods are accomplished through the pain inflicted on others. When that occurs, we run the risk of cutting the moral nerve needed to oppose suffering where it is a function of wrongdoing.

The distinctions to be made between consolation and rationalization are fragile and, under the right circumstances, far too easily exploited. One could reasonably argue, for example, that the institutionalized misery created by slavery was completely unacknowledged in some cases because it was identified as the will of God. This line of reasoning was deeply imprinted on the minds of early Americans and often cited, but the famed preacher of the Great Awakening, Jonathan Edwards, was among the most explicit:

> So you that are servants and poor negroes. You are of those who are poor in the world, but hearken to the call of Christ, and improve the present opportunity earnestly to seek your salvation. . . . Though you are a servant, yet if you will come to Christ, and heartily give up your life to his service, you shall be the Lord's freeman. . . . If you refuse to hearken to Christ, and live in the neglect of your salvation, then you will not only be the servant of men, but the servant of the devil, and will hereafter fall into his hands, and be in his possession forever.[9]

Preaching of this kind not only hardened patterns of racism that still exist today, but slowed the engagement of many churches in the Civil Rights movement. Captive to the political climate of the day, we sometimes became involved only after it was socially embarrassing not to be.

Christians cannot afford to be genteel about cases of this kind and there is clear precedent in our faith tradition for the kind of candor needed. In an increasingly complex and inter-connected world, systems will continue to foster suffering that cannot be addressed without examining our role in shaping the systems themselves. The church should be able to embrace the pain, anger, and despair of those who suffer; practice solidarity with the people who do; and oppose the causes where possible.

The Christophers, a Roman Catholic lay order, have a motto: "It is better to light a single candle than to curse the darkness." As good as it is, I believe a better motto might be "It is best both to light a single candle and to curse the darkness." Having acknowledged evil, part of the Christian response to suffering and evil should be protest and resistance.

To be of genuine value, however, that protest will require a new dimension of sophistication that weds social, economic, and political analysis with theological clarity and moral fervor. Far too much of the protest and resistance that the church practices today is marked by well-meaning naïveté or by a tendency to simply echo established political positions. We are, as a result, all but completely captive to the political climate. We become engaged when other people are politically engaged. We lose interest when others lose interest. And the theological reasons we give for our involvement hang in the air like an afterthought.

We would do well to remember that social engagement is not an alien activity or an addendum to otherwise religious responsibilities. As children of a God who brings order in the midst of chaos, our responsibility is to extend that order. An early Jewish elaboration (or midrash) on the Book of Deuteronomy says: "'So you are My witnesses—declares the Lord—and I am God.' That is, if you are My witnesses, I am God, and if you are not My witnesses, I am, as it were, not God."[10] In a similar vein, but in different language, the author of Ephesians writes:

> . . . [S]peaking the truth in love, we must grow up in every way into him who is the head, into Christ, from whom the whole body, joined and knit together by every ligament with which it is equipped, as each part is working properly, promotes the body's growth in building itself up in love. (Ephesians 4:15–16)

They Practice Being Present.

At times, however, it is important simply to be present with those who are suffering. Time and again I have heard people testify to the healing, reassuring character of someone who was willing to be prayerfully present with them at a time of loss.

There is no hint that they felt cheated because a friend had no easy or complete solution. The obverse is true as well. When any and all traces of caring are missing, people experience their greatest peril.

The reason, it seems to me, is deeply rooted in the relational world in which God has placed us. Present to one another, we extend the presence of God, meeting a need that is more basic than any we might face in the moment of suffering. The ability not only to listen, but to create a gracious space where listening can take place, is a reminder of the larger relationship we share with God, a reminder of when, in the cool of the evening, God was walking in the garden. Gone is the need to minimize our fears or to conjure up a hidden blessing. Through simple presence we experience love and acceptance—the space to "be"—whoever we are, however we are.

We should be careful, however, to avoid assuming that the benefits belong only to those who suffer. The common fabric of human life, graced by God, is one we all share. So, the wisdom acquired by those who struggle with loss can often be of far greater value to us than any words of comfort that might be offered by the "hale and hearty." The deep, careful listening we can and should do in a caring community will nurture that wisdom and appropriate it in lives lived more thoughtfully and prayerfully.

At times that listening will challenge and provoke us. We live our lives in ever-smaller communities within communities, narrowing our vision of life. Our natural inclination is to resist learning anything that might impinge upon that vision. Yet, if the stories people tell are heard as an invitation to broaden and enrich that vision, then there is learning to be done. With candor, may you be the instrument of enduring peace.

Notes

Chapter One

1. Alexandra Korff Scott, Heddy Fairbank Reid, and Frederica Isabelle Scott, *The Soul in Balance: The Gardens of Washington National Cathedral* (McLean, Va.: EPM Publications, 1998), 83.

2. See Theodore Walker, Jr., "Congregational Dancing and Black Religion" (unpublished paper presented to the faculty of Perkins School of Theology, Southern Methodist University, October 31, 2000), 4–5.

3. Jerelyn Eddings et al., "A Persistent Stealth Racism Is Poisoning Black-White Relations," *U.S. News and World Report* 119, no. 16 (October 23, 1995): 40.

4. See, e.g., Judith Wallerstein, Julia Lewis, and Sandra Blakeslee, *The Unexpected Legacy of Divorce: A 25 Year Landmark Study* (New York: Hyperion, 2000).

5. The words are those of the German mystic, Meister Eckhart, as quoted by Matthew Fox, *The Reinvention of Work, A New Vision of Livelihood for Our Time* (San Francisco: HarperSanFrancisco, 1994), 3.

6. Barbara Rudolf, *Disconnected: How Six People from AT&T Discovered the New Meaning of Work in a Downsized Corporate America* (New York: Free Press, 1998), 155ff.

7. "News Briefs," *Environmental Science and Technology* (January, 2000): 17A.

8. Lance Morrow, "Africa: The Scramble for Existence," *Time* (September 7, 1992): 41.

9. Ibid.

10. John C. Avise, *The Genetic Gods: Evolution and Belief in Human Affairs* (Cambridge: Harvard University Press, 1998), 62ff.

11. "Insurance in the Genetic Age," *The Economist* 357, no. 8193 (October 21, 2000): 23.

12. Ludwig Wittgenstein, *The Blue and Brown Books* (New York: Harper & Row, 1958), 17. See also William H. Brenner, *Wittgenstein's Philosophical Investigations* (Albany, N.Y.: State University of New York Press, 1999), 23f.

13. Marjorie Hewitt Suchocki, *The End of Evil: Process Theology in Historical Context* (Albany, N.Y.: State University of New York Press, 1988), 59.

14. Ibid., 63.

Chapter Two

1. Kenneth Cragg, *Faith and Life Negotiate: A Christian Story-Study* (Norwich, England: Canterbury Press, 1994), 1.

2. *New York Times,* 1 October 2000: A4.

3. Cable News Network, October 8, 2000.

4. *People* (April 1, 1996): 64.

5. *New York Times,* 1 October 2000: A9.

6. Ironically, this violence is described as "virtual reality" in advertisements in order to invite the purchase of video games, but when sociologists and civic leaders suggest that it might be psychologically destructive to expose our nation's children to this kind of experience, those who market the medium then defend their products by describing them using the same words, but stressing the word *virtual.*

7. Woody Allen, *Without Feathers* (New York: Random House, 1975), 99.

8. John Hick, *Evil and the God of Love,* 2d ed. (New York: Harper & Row, 1978), 7–9.

9. Barry L. Whitney, *What Are They Saying about God and Evil?* (New York: Paulist Press, 1989), 8ff.

10. Abraham Heschel, *The Prophets* (New York: Harper & Row, 1962), 308f.

11. Habakkuk 2:4b.

12. See Bruce Barron, *The Health and Wealth Gospel: What's Going On in a Movement That Has Shaped the Lives of Millions?* (Downers Grove, Ill.: InterVarsity Press, 1987).

13. Ibid., 23.

14. Granger Westerberg, "What Is Good Grief?" (address to the fourth annual Spiritual/Bereavement Seminar for Hospice Caregivers, Mansfield, Ohio, April 30, 1987).

Chapter Three

1. Rudolfo Anaya, *Bless Me, Ultima* (New York: Warner Books, 1972), 186–7.

2. In earlier versions of this material I intuitively relied on the language used below, convinced that this would make the material more readily accessible to a larger audience. In a subsequent presentation, Charles Brown, Oglesby Professor of Pastoral Theology at Union Theological Seminary, Richmond, Va., observed, "This is the way we should do theology," referring, I take it, to the language I used to summarize the personal theologies we build for ourselves. Thanks to his observation, I have made more of that emphasis here in explicit terms.

3. In 1995 Jenkins described his experience for the North American Deans' Conference held in Birmingham, England.

4. Bruce Bower, *Stealing Jesus: How Fundamentalism Betrays Christianity* (New York: Crown Publishers, 1997), 185.

5. Ibid.

6. Andrew Sung Park, *The Wounded Heart of God: The Asian Concept of Han and the Christian Doctrine of Sin* (Nashville: Abingdon, 1993), 10–14.

7. Leslie D. Weatherhead, *The Will of God* (Nashville: Abingdon, 1972), 10–11.

8. Dorothy Sayers, *Christian Letters to a Post-Christian World* (New York: Macmillan, 1978), 24.

9. Gloria Copeland, *God's Will Is Prosperity* (Tulsa, Okla.: Harrison House, 1978), 35.

10. Kenneth E. Hagin, *How to Write Your Own Ticket with God* (Tulsa, Okla.: Faith Library, 1979), 3ff.

11. Ibid.

12. See Martin Hengel, *Christ and Power,* trans. Everett R. Kalin (Philadelphia: Fortress Press, 1977), 15ff.

13. See, for example, Mark 8:27–38.

14. See Weatherhead, *Will of God,* passim.

Chapter Four

1. Whitney, *What Are They Saying about God and Evil?* 3.

2. Ibid.

3. Paul Davies, *The Mind of God: The Scientific Basis for a Rational World* (New York: Simon & Schuster, 1992), 200.

4. Some theologians have argued that a natural theology is both impossible and undesirable. In the twentieth century Emil Brunner

and Karl Barth hotly debated the issue, with Brunner defending natural theology and Barth arguing against it. Barth's arguments were summarized in a brief book, tersely entitled *Nein! Antwort an Emil Brunner* (No! An Answer to Emil Brunner) (Munich: C. Kaiser, 1934).

5. Thomas Aquinas, *Summa Theologiae*, pt. I, ques. II, art. 3.

6. William Paley, *Natural Theology: Or, Evidences of the Existence and Attributes of the Deity, Collected from the Appearances of Nature* (Boston: Gould & Lincoln, 1872), 5f.

7. Quoted in Davies, *The Mind of God*, 201.

8. Quoted in ibid.

9. Cf. Josef Pieper, *The Silence of Saint Thomas: Three Essays*, trans. John Murray and Daniel O'Connor (Chicago: Henry Regnery, 1957), 32ff. Pieper underlines the dangers inherent in Protestantism, but misses the potential difficulties in the position Aquinas takes.

10. Paul Althaus, *The Theology of Martin Luther*, trans. Robert C. Schultz (Philadelphia: Fortress Press, 1966), 17–18.

11. Roland Bainton, *Here I Stand: A Life of Martin Luther* (Nashville: Abingdon Press, 1950), 219.

12. Althaus, *Theology of Martin Luther*, 15–16 and 15 n. 3.

13. Althaus, *Theology of Martin Luther*, 17 n. 11.

14. William J. Bouwsma, *John Calvin: A Sixteenth-Century Portrait* (New York: Oxford University Press, 1988), 71f.

15. Ibid., 75.

16. John T. McNeill, "Natural Law in the Teaching of the Reformers," *Journal of Religion* 26 (1946): 168.

17. Roland H. Bainton, *Here I Stand*, 40ff.

18. Bouwsma, *John Calvin*, 49ff. In what follows I am indebted to Bouwsma's treatment, which probes the logic of Calvin's theology in a way that is missing from most works on his life and thought.

19. Ibid., 180f.

20. Ibid., 169.

21. Ibid., 170.

22. Ibid.

23. Ibid.

24. See, for example, Brian Morris, *Anthropological Studies of Religion* (Cambridge, England: Cambridge University Press, 1987), 70–71, 104–105, 146–51, 190–95; and Graham Cunningham, *Religion and Magic: Approaches and Theories* (New York: New York University Press, 1999).

25. Jacob Neusner, "Science and Magic, Miracle and Magic in Formative Judaism: The System and the Difference," in *Religion, Science, and Magic: In Concert and in Conflict,* ed. Jacob Neusner et al. (New York: Oxford University Press, 1989), 61–62.

26. Hans H. Penner, "Rationality, Ritual, and Science," in *Religion, Science, and Magic,* ed. Neusner et al., 13.

27. So, for example, J. G. Frazer, *The Golden Bough* (London: Macmillan, 1922). See also Morris, *Anthropological Studies of Religion,* 103ff.

28. Keith Thomas, *Religion and the Decline of Magic* (New York: Charles Scribner's Sons, 1971), 177.

29. Larry Dossey, *Be Careful What You Pray For . . . You Just Might Get It* (San Francisco: HarperSanFrancisco, 1997), 24–26. Emphasis mine.

30. Anne Foerst, "MIT Robot Lab Theologian Asks, 'Is Cyber Prayer Just Plain Childish?'" *Spirituality & Health* 4, no. 2 (summer 2001): 24.

31. Morris, *Anthropological Studies of Religion,* 149–50.

32. Richard Stivers, *Technology as Magic: The Triumph of the Irrational* (New York: Continuum, 1999), 4–8. See also Frances Fitzgerald, *Way Out There in the Blue: Reagan, Star Wars, and the End of the Cold War* (New York: Simon & Schuster, 2000).

33. E. G. Salmon, "Good," *New Catholic Encyclopedia,* vol. 6 (Washington, D.C.: Catholic University of America, 1967), 614–616.

34. Katherin A. Rogers, *Perfect Being Theology* (Edinburgh: Edinburgh University Press, 2000), 1.

Chapter Five

1. Donald Nicholl, *The Testing of Hearts: A Pilgrim's Journal* (London: Lamp Press, 1989), 9.

2. Walter Brueggemann, *Genesis* (Atlanta: John Knox Press, 1982), 25. Brueggemann's treatment of Genesis, though rarely quoted, is reflected throughout this chapter.

3. Ibid.

4. E. P. Sanders, *The Historical Figure of Jesus* (London: Penguin Press, 1993), 34.

5. Marcus Borg, *Conflict, Holiness, and Politics in the Teaching of Jesus,* Studies in the Bible and Early Christianity, vol. 5 (New York: Edwin Mellen Press, 1984), 123ff.

6. See Bruce Chilton, *Rabbi Jesus: An Intimate Biography* (New York: Doubleday, 2000), 17–8.

7. Cf. Jon D. Levenson, *Creation and the Persistence of Evil: The Jewish Drama of Divine Omnipotence* (San Francisco: Harper & Row, 1988), 12, passim. Levenson rightly observes:

> Two and a half millennia of Western theology have made it easy to forget that throughout the ancient Near Eastern world, including Israel, the point of creation is not the production of matter out of nothing, but rather the emergence of a stable community in a benevolent and life-sustaining order. The defeat by YHWH of the forces that have interrupted that order is intrinsically an act of creation.

8. Terence Fretheim observes:

> The creative activity in Genesis 1 is often depicted only in terms of a sovereign unilateral divine act; it is a command performance. For example, the verb *bara'*, "create," used only for the creative activity of God in the Old Testament, is so stressed that any connection between divine and human creativity is denigrated, or even denied. As a result, creatureliness tends to be viewed solely in terms of dependence and humility, even impotence. But Genesis 1 ought not be so interpreted. The common use of *'asah*, "make," with its many uses in the human sphere, makes it clear that God's creative work is not without analogy. Moreover, Genesis 1 speaks of creation as both mediate and immediate, indirect and indirect. In v. 11, the earth is commanded to bring forth vegetation, and it does; in v. 24 it is commanded to bring forth living creatures, and it does so. While v. 25 states that God made the beasts, the nondivine involvement cannot be explained away. . . . This dual agency is evident also in the ongoing activity of creation, witnessed elsewhere in the OT. Thus, while Ps. 104:14 testifies to God's making the grass and plants grow, Hag. 1:10–11 speaks of the ground itself bringing forth such vegetation, and of the earth withholding its produce. The latter passage also speaks of the heavens withholding the rains, while Job 37:6 makes it clear that God is responsible for *every* shower or snowfall. Other passages (e.g., Deut. 28:4 and Ps. 65:9–11, 12–13) also

make clear that blessings are due not solely to divine activity, but to a sharing of that creative power with the created order itself. In the natural order, then, there is neither a "letting go" of the creation on God's part, nor a retention of all such powers unto God. The texts reveal that creative powers are shared.

The Suffering of God: An Old Testament Perspective (Philadelphia: Fortress Press, 1984), 73–74.

9. Levenson, *Creation and the Persistence of Evil,* 10.

10. As quoted in Levenson, *Creation and the Persistence of Evil,* 15. For a lengthy treatment of still other examples, see 14ff.

11. Hosea 1:8–10. The words of v. 7 are part of a later gloss, but underline the way in which v. 6 is no doubt meant to be read. Hans Walter Wolff observes: "[I]t admonishes the reader to view the threatening verses of this chapter in terms of the entire saving history" (*Hosea: A Commentary on the Book of the Prophet Hosea, Hermeneia,* ed. Frank Moore Cross, trans. Gary Stansell (Philadelphia: Fortress Press, 1974), 21. I.e., "[T]he Yahweh who acts in the present and future is one other than the one who has begun his covenantal history with Israel at the time of her youth, with the exodus from Egypt (2:17[15]; 11:1; 13:4); with the making of the covenant (1:9; 6:7; 8:1); and with the gift of divine law (2:21f [19f]; 8:12; 13:4f). Hosea views Israel's present and future together with her history" (xxvi).

12. 1 John 4:8.

13. E.g., Mark's Gospel, especially 8:31ff.

14. E.g., Hebrews 4:14ff.

15. Philippians 2:5ff. Cf. John F. Haught, *God after Darwin: A Theology of Evolution* (Boulder, Colo.: Westview Press, 2000), 109ff.

16. Again, see Hebrews 4:14ff.

17. The Apostles' Creed begins: "I believe in God, the Father almighty, maker of heaven and earth. . . ." The opening line of the Nicene Creed strikes the same note: "We believe in one God, the Father, the Almighty, maker of heaven and earth, of all that is, seen and unseen." See *The Book of Common Prayer* (Chicago: Seabury Press, 1978), 66 and 326–7.

18. Nikos Kazantzakis, *The Last Temptation of Christ,* trans. P. A. Bien (New York: Simon & Schuster, 1960).

19. The story is one that I heard years ago by Dr. David Seamands. This version is my own paraphrase. On the larger story of Harley's work in Liberia, see J. Tremaine Copplestone, *The Methodist Episcopal*

Church, 1896–1939, vol. 4 of *History of Methodist Missions: Twentieth Century Perspectives* (New York: Board of Global Ministries of the United Methodist Church, 1973), 899–903, 909–12.

20. Henri Nouwen, *Letter of Consolation* (San Francisco: Harper & Row, 1982), 75–76, italics mine.

21. See Paul Fiddes, *The Creative Suffering of God* (Oxford: Clarendon Press, 1988), 230ff.

22. During our struggle with infertility one friend had a newsletter sent to us published specifically for those struggling with the problems we were facing. Some of the newsletter was of indifferent quality, all of it was poignant. A large part of what I am about to "affirm" about human suffering is indebted to that brief paragraph, although I have also taken the liberty to change and expand on much of it as well.

23. Nouwen, *Letter of Consolation,* 41 and 52.

24. As J. Christiaan Beker observes:

The claim that all things work for good for those who love God (v. 28) must be understood in its pregnant apocalyptic sense: even all hostile powers are within God's *final* control, and thus they serve his ultimate purpose. The predestination language in Rom. 8:29–30 is not philosophical speculation about "beginnings," or a theory of speculative theodicy; instead it functions as a *retrospective* grounding of the apocalyptic glory of God" (italics mine).

Paul the Apostle: The Triumph of God in Life and Thought (Philadelphia: Fortress Press, 1980), 365–66.

25. Cf. Paul Fiddes, who observes:

Above all, then, we depend upon the story of the suffering of God which comes to a focus in the story of Jesus. Here comes to visibility a suffering which has a purposeful content, in compassion for humankind and hope of life through death. So we can choose our suffering as a suffering with Christ. . . . If, however, we follow this line of thought we must be careful to notice two factors. Firstly, there is no question of finding a meaning that already and inherently lies behind an instance of human suffering, as if we could trace a reason why God has "sent" suffering to someone. To think like this would be to go back to the idea of a God who inflicts suffering rather than one who endures it himself; it would be to revert to an authority-figure to whose omnipotent choice, in this case a choice of meaning, we must simply submit. Rather the power of the story of divine suffering is that we can find a meaning *for* our suffering rather than one *behind* it; that is our suffering can acquire a meaning. We can put the word of the cross alongside our apparently senseless suffering, or the suffering of others, and then we can see what meaning emerges.

Creative Suffering of God, 147–48.

26. Walter Brueggemann puts it this way: "Truth has an alliance with hurt and where that alliance does not exist, the truth is suspect." From an unpublished paper read to the annual meeting of the Anglican Association of Biblical Scholars, Nashville, Tenn., November 2000.

Chapter Six

1. Bill Williams, *Naked before God: The Return of a Broken Disciple* (Harrisburg, Pa.: Morehouse, 1998), 32–33.

2. Therese A. Rando, *Treatment of Complicated Mourning* (Champaign, Ill.: Research Press, 1993), 20–21.

3. The phrase is Thomas Attig's and captures a portion of the central thesis of his book: *How We Grieve.* (New York: Oxford University Press, 1996).

4. E.g., Rando, *Treatment of Complicated Mourning,* 26. However, in even the best of the literature on the subject, the use of words varies. I am more interested in the differences represented than in the vocabulary one might use, so I have chosen to omit any rationale that might be given for one use or another of the words involved.

5. Rando, *Treatment of Complicated Mourning,* 393ff. Rando actually prefers the word *process,* but even this word, it seems to me, suggests a linear notion that is akin to *stages* or *phases.* She safeguards against this misunderstanding by taking considerable time to explain what she means by the word *process;* because she is writing for clinicians, it works well in that context.

6. The definitions are outlined at length by Rando, *Treatment of Complicated Mourning,* 11ff.

7. Ibid., 149ff.

8. See Kenneth Doka, *Disenfranchised Grief: Recognizing Hidden Sorrow* (Lexington, Mass.: Lexington Books, 1989); and Ben Wolfe,

"AIDS and Bereavement: Special Issues in Spiritual Counseling," in *Death and Spirituality*, ed. Kenneth J. Doka with John D. Morgan (Amityville, N.Y.: Baywood Publishing, 1993), 257ff.

9. Ibid., 34.

10. Ibid., 139.